Pete's Story

Pete's Story

Rachel Jackson

Authentic

First published 2000 by Eagle Publishing Ltd.
Reprinted 2012 by Authentic Media Limited
52 Presley Way, Crownhill, Milton Keynes. MK8 0ES
www.authenticmedia.co.uk

British Library Cataloguing in Publication Data
A catalogue record for this book is available from the British Library.

ISBN-13: 978-1-86024-545-9

Cover design by fourninezero design.
Printed and bound by CPI Group (UK) Ltd, Croydon, CR0 4YY.

Many people were told, by God, that the apostle Paul would have trouble if he went to Jerusalem. They begged him not to go, but Paul replied, *'You're looking at this backwards. The issue in Jerusalem is not what they do to me, whether arrest or murder, but what the Master Jesus does through my obedience. Can't you see that?'*

Acts 21:13 (The Message)

Dedicated to all Pete's friends and family but, above all, to our only wise God, that it may be used to his glory.

Contents

Acknowledgements

I was only able to write this book because of the wealth of help given by so many friends. They encouraged me – sometimes like King Harold as illustrated in the Bayeaux Tapestry at the Battle of Hastings, with the point of a spear – and prayed for me. If I were to list all of you I would need another chapter, but special thanks to Annie Montifiore and Lynda Neillands who read the manuscript and ejected loads of woolly matter, for the encouragement and help from our family and most of all to my incredible husband Julian, for his loving, godly wisdom, patience, fortitude and hundreds of cups of coffee.

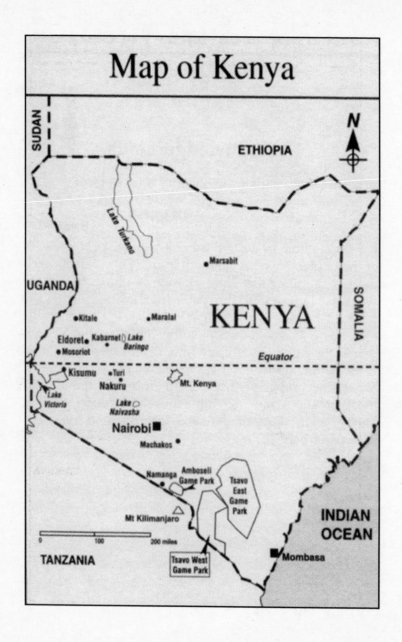

Map of Kenya

N

SUDAN

ETHIOPIA

Lake Turkana

•Marsabit

UGANDA

KENYA

SOMALIA

•Kitale   •Maralal

Eldoret• Kabarnet○ *Lake Baringo*
•Mosoriot

Equator

•Kisumu   •Turi
Lake Victoria   Nakuru   ○ Mt. Kenya

Lake Naivasha ○

Nairobi ■

Machakos •

Namanga • Amboseli Game Park   Tsavo East Game Park

△ Mt Kilimanjaro

0   100   200 miles

TANZANIA

Tsavo West Game Park

■ Mombasa

INDIAN OCEAN

A Sketch Map of the Territory of East Pokot

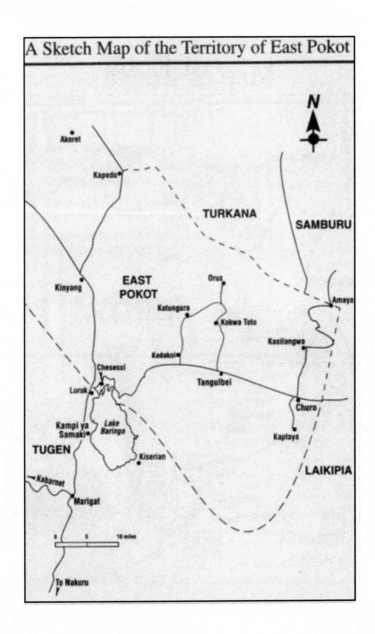

CRISIS

I shall be satisfied, when I awake with
thy likeness.
Psalm 17:15, KJV

I love you O LORD my strength.
Psalm 18:1

1

Mlam Tich

Pete Jackson came jumping and sliding down the hillside above Orus, skilfully avoiding the thorn bushes and boulders. Apart from the sound of his descent, the only noises were the occasional cry of a bird and dislodged stones rattling down ahead of him.

Though he was wearing only khaki shorts and his elderly Kenyan safari boots, he was exceedingly hot. His bronze hair over his oval face looked redder than usual in the afternoon light. Much recent physical exertion had made his clear features more defined: the long nose he had inherited from his mother's side of the family; the square chin from his father's. But his most noticeable features were his eyes, green like his father's and always smiling. His tan was patchy, for it was chiefly the result of the merging of hundreds of freckles, especially over his shoulders.

Slung around his neck was an old bag containing his journal and his patchwork-covered Study Bible, his binoculars, and his precious Pentax camera – an eighteenth-birthday present from his family. Pentax would not have recognised it in its elongated bag

made of odd bits of cloth. It was elongated for extra
protection, extra films and also as a disguise for when
he would be travelling on buses during August – not
long now!

Pete felt pleased. That morning he and Reuben, the
local pastor, had finished clearing the track through the
thorn bushes from Kokwo Toto to missionaries Art and
Mary Ellen Davis's small house here in Orus, so that their
Land Rover would be able to get in without too many
problems the next day. He had spent this, his last free
afternoon, on his favourite hill being quiet and taking a
series of photos that would look good in his university
room. Now he was heading farther down the valley to
spend his last evening with Reuben and his wife, Esther.
Tomorrow, after greeting the Davises and their guests,
Pete would be heading back to the centre (in Kenya, any
location where there is an infrastructure such as a school,
shops, chief's post, etc. is usually called a 'centre') at
Kokwo Toto where he was living.

He could already smell Esther's charcoal fire below
in the valley. Soon he was vaulting the cow fence of
sticks tied together with withers. Reuben was sitting in
the lean-to veranda outside his half-finished house. He
certainly deserved a rest; it had been heavy work that
morning moving the rocks that the rain and cows had
unearthed.

'*Sera nyoman*, Pete!' Reuben called out the Pokot
greeting. 'You had a good climb? How was *Mlam Tich*
[The place where the-cows-never-go-hungry]? Could
you see anything from up there?'

'*Sera nyoman*, Reuben!' Pete smiled. 'It was good. And
I saw smoke coming from the place where you thought
those people lived, the ones we wanted to visit. Even
their cows are back. I heard them lowing. So when can
we visit them?'

They sat outside for a while, enjoying playing with 2-year-old Cheses, the evening bird sounds and the smell of supper being cooked in the outside kitchen. They could hear Reuben's cows too, just over the other side of the hollow, as the herd boy, Paulo Kakuko, brought them back to their *boma* (byre) before nightfall. Everything was so peaceful again after the recent scares.

Orus lay in a valley amongst the hills at the northern end of Kenya's Rift Valley, where the savannah and forests further south have turned into low thorn bushes and scrub. Reuben and Esther were East Pokot, one of the pastoral nomadic peoples of the region.

There was a history of cattle raiding between the Pokot and their neighbours the Turkana. There had been ten years of peace, but recently new tensions had arisen. The Orus women and the cows had been taken to a safer place, but now the scare had passed and the full moon – the season of raids – was over. The women and children were back.

Paulo finished securing the cows in their *boma* and joined Reuben and Pete. Because of the mosquitoes they went into the living room to have their supper.

'Pete, were you dreaming again last night?' asked Paulo. 'I didn't hear you call out in your sleep.'

'No,' replied Pete, 'I don't remember last night. But you must be a good sleeper. Twice this last week I've woken myself up with calling out. Yes, you must have been sound asleep – it must be the heat!'

After their last cup of sweet tea, they sat and prayed together, as was their custom. That night it was Esther's turn to pray for them all. Then Pete and Paulo crossed back over the dry stream bed to a metal *rondavel* (a prefabricated round metal hut, as used by the Roads Department) where they were sleeping, near the cattle *boma,* and Reuben and Esther went thankfully to bed in their house, glad that all the preparations were complete for the arrival of Art and Mary Ellen and their visitors the next day.

Tomorrow, Art and Mary Ellen were to attend the opening of the large new church the President had built at Kabartonjo, 190 kilometres down the valley. Many people would be attending. But Reuben was not going. Esther needed care these days. She was carrying their second 'special' baby – special because they had been cursed by relatives who had declared that because they were Christians they would be childless. They had waited twelve years for the wonderful day that Cheses had been born.

'The meeting should be over by midday. The Davises will arrive before dark,' he thought thankfully, as they turned out the small hurricane lamp.

They were completely unaware that the entire area was full of silent men.

At 5 o'clock in the morning, a sixth sense woke Reuben. He knew that something was badly wrong. There were men outside his house, and they were speaking in the Turkana language. He put his shoes on, but quickly realised that the whole valley was full of cattle thieves. There was nothing he could do. It would be suicidal to try to protect his cows. He made Esther and Cheses hide under a bed and joined them himself. He was certain that they were going to be killed.

'Esther,' he whispered, 'we are going to heaven now.'

There was a burst of gunfire over the Davises' house. Next, to his horror, he heard the breaking of metal from the *rondavel* and loud Turkana exclamations from that direction. There were two further bursts of gunfire, followed by a great cry. Sick at heart, he lay under the bed and listened to the men speaking angrily outside the hut.

Three hundred Turkana were moving down the valley, taking with them hundreds of stolen cows. There was nothing for it but to wait for daylight.

2

'He Set My Feet Upon a Rock'

Art and Mary Ellen set out early, with cheerful hearts, for Kabartonjo. It was a very special day. Kabartonjo was the place where the President of Kenya, Daniel Arap Moi, had attended a missionary primary school and had first heard of Jesus. In thanks to God he had now had a beautiful church built there, able to accommodate 2,000 people – it was almost a cathedral. That Sunday, 21st July 1992, was to be its official opening. Church leaders and missionaries from all over the country would be attending. Art and Mary Ellen Davis had marked the date on their calendar a long time ago. They were bringing with them fellow missionaries Peter and Mary McCallum, and some American visitors. They all planned to drive on to stay at Orus for at least a week after the opening ceremony.

After the long, straight road from Nakuru, the party turned west, driving up the side of the Tugen range, a steep hill road with hairpin bends (but mercifully now all tarmac) to the town of Kabarnet. This is the centre of the Tugen district, the home of the Tugen people group. At Kabarnet they turned north again, following the crest of the range, on another tarmac road through an area part forest and part Tugen smallholdings. The countryside was green and beautiful after the recent rain, the fields of maize already knee-high. They continued on to Kabartonjo and found large crowds already arriving, either by foot or small pick-up truck, many singing as they came.

The church and political leaders, who had already arrived, welcomed them. It was a long but joyful service, with many speakers, including the President himself, giving thanks to God for the new building. Afterwards the President had arranged a banquet in the hotel in Kabarnet. The Davises and the McCallums had been invited. Feeling very honoured, they joined the other guests at the hotel.

The two families had been allocated different tables at the banquet. Suddenly, the McCallums saw Art Davis crossing the room towards them. Art was ashen-faced.

'Someone has just arrived from Churo. Peter, I can't believe what he's told me. There was another Turkana raid in Orus last night. Five people were killed – including Pete Jackson.'

3

'All We Have . . . Then Bring Them Here to Me'

The McCallums immediately drove back up the valley to Eldama Ravine, a small town where a kind Catholic priest had already taken the wounded and Pete's body to the simple Catholic hospital. The Pokot dead would be buried by their families in the hills. Peter went to the hospital to confirm that the body really was that of Pete Jackson. It was.

Thankfully, there were other AIM missionary friends living in the town. (When missionaries first went to Kenya, the different sending societies wisely decided to divide up the work between them. This area was the one covered by the Africa Inland Mission, now AIM International. The Davises and the McCallums were AIM missionaries.) Peter and Mary went to their house to try to telephone – it is often a difficult task in up-country Kenya to get a good connection. The missionaries' telephone had been inoperative for a month, but that day it had begun working again. Soon urgent telephone calls had been made to Nakuru, Nairobi and England.

Art and Mary Ellen, with heavy hearts, began the journey back to Orus.

In England it was a glorious midsummer Sunday. At our home in Kent we, Pete's parents, decided not to go to our own church that morning. We usually commuted twenty-five miles to Emmanuel, South Croydon (the church that had prayed for us and supported us for many years), on the few Sundays that we were at home. But that Sunday we had attended our local Baptist church, as Rosalyn (Rozi), our daughter, was coming down from London for the day, and James Foot, a pupil from Tonbridge School, was also visiting us. After lunch, we went for a walk in the woods, which were dappled with sunlight and alive with blackbird song. We returned to make an early tea, as Rozi had to get back to London.

The telephone jolted us. My husband, Julian, answered it. Suddenly he staggered backwards. I rushed over to him, thinking he was having a heart attack.

'It's Pete. He's been killed.'

We stood shocked, honoured, stricken, stunned.

Julian and I had worked with the Africa Inland Mission in East Africa for over thirty years. We had only returned to England in May. Peter, our youngest son, generally known as Pete, had been staying with us in Nairobi in April and had gone on to Orus as a volunteer for a three-month stint before returning to England and university in October.

The phone jarred us again. It was Pete's friend, Chris Foot – James's brother – phoning from Kenya.

'*Pole.*' (The Swahili word is an expression of deep sympathy.) 'But lucky him – he's got there first. I have a verse for you: Philippians 3:21. That describes Pete.'

We hurried to get a Bible to look it up. We were desperate to hear something from God. The phone went again.

'It's Chris again. I meant chapter 1, not 3. We're praying for you.'

We read the verse. *'For me to live is Christ and to die is gain'* – overwhelming encouragement. 'But make it real for us, Lord!' we cried.

Then the letters and cards came pouring in.

I resented them at first. I just wanted to forget. But as we read them, we wept and wept. We were overwhelmed by the love people showed us. So many were praying for us; and we were conscious of it, and of being lifted up in spirit.

But we were deeply perplexed. Why Pete? We loved him dearly. We felt that he had not had time to achieve very much. If only he'd had longer, he could have been used by the Holy Spirit to help many others to find God. And were we wrong to allow him to go to that place? So we were overawed by what we read in the letters of what God had allowed him to do, and of God's timing.

Also, the Lord of heaven's armies had not left us entirely unprepared. God had left things around for us to read. In a friend's house, three weeks before all this, I had idly read C.S. Lewis's *Till We Have Faces: A Myth Retold*[1] which shows how God has much bigger plans than we can imagine when he takes somebody special. And just the week before, Julian had read to me a quotation he had copied down before we were married. It was from a book by Jonathan Goforth, a missionary to China. He wrote of the Boxer uprising in China, in which many Christians had been killed.

> While still unable to answer the 'WHY', we saw our almighty God used his own prerogative to glorify his name, whether in the glorious martyrdom of some or in the miraculous deliverance of others.[2]

Although we were shattered, these words were strangely comforting.

Soon after Pete's death, the editor of our mission's magazine asked us to write an article about him. We felt we could not do so at that time. However, as the months passed, various incidents nudged me towards writing: a retired missionary wrote from Canada and asked for anything I had written about Pete; a woman I didn't know very well sent us £10 towards writing a book. I was still very loath to do so, as it seemed rather a sentimental thing to do. And when I mentioned the idea to one of our other sons, he said sadly, 'Well, there isn't much to write.'

And so I thought, too, at first.

The following year, AIM International asked us to take meetings in the south-east of England to promote prayer for Africa. I spoke many times about the story of the feeding of the 5,000, explaining how the little that we give to the Lord in prayer can be so multiplied by him.

One day I was praying and I read the story again, from John's Gospel. Suddenly, in that extraordinary way that God works, I saw that the lad with the loaves and fishes was Pete with his journals and letters. I was to give them up to the Lord and he would use them to bless many. There were other confirmations too. So that is why this book has been written: it is not something that I desired to write for the sake of writing a book, and I feel that its purpose is not to just perpetuate the memory of Pete Jackson, but for something much bigger from God.

Once, long ago, I had been cheerfully and sincerely praying through Paul's letter in the Bible to the Philippians. I read:

'I want to know Christ –' Yes, Lord! *'– and the power of his resurrection –'* That would be so good, Father! *'– and the fellowship of his sufferings –'* . . . Oh!

I cannot claim we have known that fellowship yet: perhaps just a tiny edge of the threshold – tiny, but very precious.

John Bunyan said that when he was thrown into prison for preaching the gospel, he kept looking for Scripture to 'stand on'. I think this was my greatest desire after Pete died. I scrambled through people's letters to see if they had something for me of rebuke or encouragement. One, from a young friend of ours who had been at school with Pete, was immensely strengthening. *'He reached down from on high and took hold of me; he drew me out of deep waters'* (Psalm 18:16). She also said that God had given her a number and she felt it must be a page in her Bible. On that page was the story of Jacob's dream. 'I felt that for Pete, he would've had a glorious ascent into God's shimmering presence.'

We sat at breakfast with the letter, weeping with joy.

As Bunyan said, 'To die is not death.' Pete came to this slowly. This is his story that God planned for him.

STAGE 1

The LORD is my rock . . .
my God is my rock, in whom I take refuge.
Psalm 18:2

4

Kapruandet and Kiptanui

For my husband and me, 1970 was a year of new beginnings. After nearly ten years in a teacher training college near the Ugandan border, we had felt strongly that we should do something to help national Christians in business and the professions, for who at that time there was minimal pastoral care.

The obvious place to start was Nairobi. We had returned there from England following a time of sadness and growth. Julian's father had died, and we had lost a precious baby when I was four months pregnant. But we had learnt as a couple to talk and share together as never before. Now back in Nairobi, we had moved into a guesthouse, after (with much heart searching) putting our two older children, Jonathan and Rozi, into boarding school, and Colin into a nursery school, while we went on a course to improve our Kiswahili language skills and started house-hunting.

It was certainly new beginnings. We had never lived in a city before; we had never tried to buy a house before. We took our first ever holiday in Mombasa, on the coast. And Julian was asked to try a new job as pastor, instead of teacher, at a new English-language service that had been started at a large church in the suburbs, for there were so many educated Kenyans who preferred English to Swahili.

Julian spent much time in prayer.

One day, to his surprise – apparently out of the blue – God used Bible verses about new babies to make him wonder whether God might be telling us to try again for a fourth child. Julian did not tell me this directly, but suggested I spent a morning in prayer. Afterwards he asked me,

'Did the Lord tell you anything special?'

I mentioned one or two things, but not about babies. However, a few weeks before, a verse in a book of daily readings, from 1 Chronicles 22, had stuck out from the rest of the page. It said, 'A son shall be born to thee, who shall be a man of rest.' I had thought, 'Well, if this means anything, Lord, you tell Julian.'

First, we needed a house. We had already decided that a mortgage was preferable to paying heavy rent. At that time the mission had very little housing in Nairobi, so we had been asked to find our own accommodation because both we and the mission felt certain that God wanted us there in that city.

After an exhausting and sometimes fractious time checking many house agents and houses, we at last decided to have a morning of prayer, following a suggestion from an old friend, Joe Mullins, who had visited us from India. It was holiday time, so we farmed out Jonathan and Rozi for the morning and took the telephone off the hook. We prayed, wept and asked each other's forgiveness for our irritability. Then, at noon, when Julian had gone to collect Colin from nursery school, I opened *The Standard* (a Kenyan national newspaper) and saw an advertisement for a bungalow in Riverside Drive.

I drove over there that afternoon with Rozi. The wife let us in by the back kitchen door. Even the door delighted us; it was a split door, like a stable's. There was an old-fashioned, trustworthy gas stove in the first kitchen, then one entered the second kitchen which was full of cupboards and an ironing table (Kenyans usually prefer a table to iron on rather than the little board Westerners use), with a serving hatch into the dining room. But I think it was when she opened the next door, into the dining room, that I thought, 'Lord, is this your answer for us?'

There were two large rooms, divided by beautiful curtains. Beyond was another smaller room that you could look through to the driveway. To the right was a small toilet and then a glass door leading into a little passage, off which were the bathroom and two bedrooms. The larger of the two bedrooms had more glass doors, with lilac-flowered curtains, leading to another little room facing the front of the house where a baby was asleep; the smaller had its own shower and toilet 'en suite', as the agent's blurb put it.

We stepped back into the garden. A high trellis, covered with coral plant and roses and overhung with a huge avocado tree, divided the back yard from the rest of the garden. It was like a secret garden. We went through the archway into a fair-sized vegetable garden. Then on the left was a path that divided, one way down to a small water garden (from the waste shower water) and a rockery, and the other way past another high trellis, covered with breathtaking blue petrea, into a rose garden and beyond to the lawns in front of the house, which were surrounded on two sides by trees, bougainvilleas and other beautiful shrubs. The house, we learned, had been on the market for some time. The owners were an Indian family who wanted to leave for Canada, so they had just drastically lowered the price.[3]

The following day, Julian and I sat in the sitting-room with the owners, discussing the price. By 'mistake' the agent brought another viewer round while we were there. The man looked very interested. Julian made a decision.

'We'd like to buy it, please.'

The following day at the lawyer's office, the Indian gentleman said, 'If you not here when I come, I pick up phone to the other man. He offered me one thousand more than you. But I say, "I promise Mr Jackson," so we come.'

We gasped in awe at what God had done.

Long before, my father had called his first house 'Rock House'. As our down payment had been made possible by money he had left us, we felt that it would be a good name for our house too. We translated it into Kalenjin, one of the Kenyan languages: *Kapruandet* – literally 'the place of the rock': the 'Rock', because that's a name Moses, Hannah, David and others used for God, our only foundation for life. We had the name painted onto a sign for the gate, but decided that it might confuse our visitors. So instead we followed the Kenyan custom of putting our name outside the gate: 'J.H. Jackson'.

We moved in during October, with great joy. It was Jonathan and Rozi's school half-term. They brought with them two Ugandan school friends who were unable to go home for half-term. The house was filled with joyful shouts and laughter from the very beginning. We were very thankful that the retiring principal of the language school we had attended had asked if anyone needed a cook and general house person, as the man they employed needed another job. (It is the custom in all Kenyan households to have someone, possibly a cousin or younger sister, to help with the housework. These people become part of your family.)

We took James on for three months' probation – he lived with us in his bedsit at the back of the house for twenty years! We praise God for him. He cooked and cleaned for us, and prepared thousands of cups of tea for exhausted refugees.

One day the following September, Julian had taken little Colin for a walk; I was resting, as I was now expecting our fourth child. Suddenly I noticed huge storm clouds blowing up. I grabbed mackintoshes and hurried down our drive, still in my go-to-church heels, to meet them. I slipped on the cobbled road, fell flat on my face, and lay there full of fear for our baby. A kindly Kenyan gentleman who was passing helped me to my feet, and I limped home again, so ashamed of my carelessness. But the Lord had his hand over that child and kept him.

In December, Julian rushed me into Nairobi hospital; although I was only just over eight months pregnant, I had started to bleed. I was immediately confined to bed. On Sunday morning, when the surgeon came to see me, I was taken aback when he remarked,

'My operating day is Tuesday. I want to investigate this child under anaesthetic before you start labour.'

'Oh dear – that's not very convenient for my husband. Our conference starts that day.'

'Well, we could do it today,' he replied. 'I will get the secretary to contact your husband.'

Julian was at a large church called Ziwani, where he was now responsible for the English service. It was

a special day: the Africa Inland Church's theological
college (called Scott College, after the mission's founder,
Peter Cameron Scott) was holding its graduation there.
Julian, as an official Ziwani pastor, was on the platform.
Thankfully, Colin was with friends for the day. Jonathan
and Rozi were at boarding school. It really was a miracle
that eventually someone heard the church telephone.
The hospital secretary had been trying on and off for
hours to get through.

As soon as Julian got the message, he rushed to
the hospital, going up the stairs two at a time to the
operating theatre. A nursing sister stopped him.

'Are you Mr Jackson? Look at this!' she laughed,
showing him a tiny damp child in a blanket. She was
on her way to put him in an incubator for the night.

A boy! And we had only chosen girls' names!

Julian, knowing I would be out for a while, staggered
back to collect Colin and take him home to bath him.
At that time, Colin was deep into the adventures of
Peter and Jane in his reading book at nursery school
and his best friend was Peter Kanyi.

'Let's call him Peter, Dad!'

The next day we decided that we could not think of
a better name. So Peter it was, with two family names
added so that he could be found in the London telephone
book! As we had previously been working amongst
the Nandi people, he needed a Nandi name too: either
the time he was born, or something significant that
happened then. *Kiprono* (the-boy-born-when-the-goats-
are-led-home) could have been right, but talking it over
with other Nandi women we felt *Kiptanui* (the-boy-who-
nearly-died) would be better. Besides the September
fall, I had been rushed into hospital in October due
to bleeding. A small prayer group which met that
evening had asked God to heal me. Remarkably, as I

am inclined to bleed rather profusely, I had stopped immediately. And on that Sunday in December when the surgeon examined me he found that the umbilical cord was so tightly wrapped round the baby's neck that had I gone into labour he might have been strangled. He also discovered that I had a condition known as placenta praevia. Had I been having this baby in my great-grandmother's time or been having my baby out in the bush, both of us would have died.

Fifteen days later, Julian came to take us home to a huge welcome that the family had prepared for us. It was with a tremendous sense of joy and profound thankfulness that we drove under the heavy arch of bougainvillaea supported by an African lilac tree, through the new white gates at the end of our drive, into Kapruandet with our 'Little Rock' (Peter means a small rock or boulder).

5

'Prepare the Way for the Lord'

Pete was adored by his sister and two brothers – but such was their love and enjoyment of him, he nearly didn't survive till Christmas.

One afternoon, I had lain down for a few minutes before I knew Pete would wake for his 'lunch'. He was in his pram near our bedroom window. Julian was hurrying back to the office but, knowing that I was tired, told the children, 'Let Mum sleep. Just push Pete around a bit if he wakes.'

I woke up half an hour later wondering why Pete was so quiet and went out to the pram. No baby there. I looked up, puzzled, to see Jonathan and Rozi swinging a big blanket at the end of the garden.

'Where's Pete?'

'Oh, he's OK, Mum. He wouldn't keep quiet while we were racing the pram round the garden, so we're swinging him in this blanket. He loves it! He's quite quiet now.'

As I grabbed him back, I thanked God again for his angels.

Later, when they were at school, I put Pete to kick on a blanket on the lawn, while I went back and forth between garden and house attending to various matters. Then I sat down in the garden to do some sewing. I heard a splash, and idly looked towards the fishpond. To my horror, there was a very large bedraggled 'goldfish' that had slipped over the edge into the water. Ten minutes before, I had been in the house. Pete had never moved so far before. He was certainly keeping up to his name, Kiptanui.

There were no 'instant' nappies in those days so for convenience he wore a nightgown at night. As he learned to walk, he would toddle round the house in it in the mornings. James the cook loved him in it and called him 'the Bishop' – a name that stuck.

Jonathan and Rozi's boarding primary school was 130 miles from Nairobi. We had put them there because we did not know the schools in Nairobi very well, and St Andrew's school, Turi was a Christian school where Jonathan had been very happy when we were still at the Teacher's College near Eldoret. We always collected them at half-term and went up to visit them on their special visiting days every few weeks, but Colin was still with us in Nairobi. He had moved up to 'proper school' the term after Pete was born, and so was around quite a bit, but of course there were large parts of the day when Pete was alone with James and me in the house. But he was a very self-contained child, with a huge imagination.

We read to the children a great deal, especially on the long car journeys, so he had plenty of ideas to build on. I didn't have to play with him all the time as I did with the others, as he was often 'being a dog or horse' or organising huge farms with his pretend friends. He had about six of these, especially 'Big John'. Or he would be with James the cook, or sliding down the side of our patient Labrador, Annabel, whom he loved. Our neighbours remember that he would follow her over to their house if we forgot to shut the white gates. Our friends thought he was charming and placid, but he was actually a very sensitive little fellow. Even as a baby, if you looked at him without smiling he would start to cry because he thought you were cross. He was very frightened of pinching ants and one friend remembers him as a toddler, weeping when monkeys came close to the car in the game park. And if he was excited at bedtime, he could not settle to sleep.

Every evening we would tell him Bible stories, show him Bible pictures and pray. He loved it. One day I found him with tears in his eyes. He had found a picture of Jesus on the cross. I had to quickly show him another one of Jesus risen and alive.

He went to Ziwani church with us from his first Christmas Day, when I sat near the door with his Moses basket swathed in mosquito net. But when he started crawling and toddling, things became more difficult. I would sit on the back step of the church with other mums or helpers. That, in turn, made me think afresh about an idea the Lord had given me, of starting an English-language Sunday school during the service. Many families came by bus or car from a distance and missed the earlier, Swahili, one. In God's mercy and with the help of many others, it proved very valuable.

Pete's favourite possession, which he always had to have when he went to bed, was a blue stuffed rabbit that had once been Colin's. Woe betide us if we forgot Bun-bun when travelling anywhere! But when Julian had to fly to England because his mother was very ill, Pete solemnly toddled in with his precious Bun-bun and told Dad to take Bun-bun to England with him; he was sure that he would cheer Grannie up. Pete had a very loving nature right from the beginning.

6

Trip to England: 'My Chosen Instrument'

Pete was very slow to learn to speak. I consoled myself with the knowledge that Einstein is believed not to have spoken until he was four; then he started with whole sentences. Pete's trouble was that he could easily make himself understood without ordinary words. His most famous sentence was, when rushing in from the garden,

'*Mum-mum come! Quack quack nyum-nyum Mum-mums bubum nyum-nyums!*' (Mummy come! Birds – are eating – your – little vegetables.)

He was completely ambidextrous. I asked his nursery school teacher to help him use his right hand, but she had a large class and I think she forgot. He grew up left-handed.

One thing that his teacher noticed, which later baffled and annoyed other teachers, was that when she gathered her class round her for an announcement or a story, Pete would just go on fiddling with some toy, apparently oblivious to what was going on. 'But,' she said, 'I don't try to stop him now, as I find he is taking everything in and can tell me all I have said.'

But I am jumping too far ahead in my story. When Pete was only 18 months old, we went on leave to England. It was a time when our lives were completely changed.

Friends had made their house in Croydon available to us. First, however, we went for a holiday in Cornwall, where Julian's mother joined us for a week. There, calamities hit us.

We were of course already very tired from travelling. Then, after drinking a cup of strong coffee and lifting a suitcase, Julian developed a very fast heartbeat. This was hard to hide from Mother for the rest of the holiday – she herself had a bad heart and was inclined to worry – but we managed it by Julian taking her out for gentle walks while I dashed round doing housework, taking the children down the cliff to the beach, and other chores. Soon I was exhausted. Then, on the last day of the holiday, Colin contracted very serious pneumonia. We had a hair-raising trip back to Surrey, and a chaotic time followed. We had to move into our friends' house, put Jonathan into a boarding school (very painful, and we had to buy his uniform as far away as Maidstone!), arrange a day school for Rozi, and while all that was going on we had to give that active child, Colin, bed-rest for three months. How thankful I was that Pete was a biddable child!

Julian was often away speaking for the mission, and was still unwell. Then a cheerful doctor friend said he would give me an injection for the superficial arteries on my leg – it caused an abscess. At the same time, I had toothache. A local harassed dentist took out the wrong tooth; I had to go back to our old dentist to have the correct one extracted. Jonathan was very unhappy at school. And Grannie, Julian's mother, was coming for Christmas.

By the time we went to the annual AIM International young people's conference in January, I was completely drained. I sat with Pete (who had a very heavy cold) in our bedroom in the Herne Bay Conference Centre for most of the weekend wondering, 'Lord, what are you trying to tell me?'

I only remember two activities from that conference that I managed to go to. One was a Bible study. The speaker said, 'If you saw a sailing ship becalmed in the middle of the ocean, wouldn't you think the sailors were foolish if they didn't put up the sails when they heard the wind coming?'

I remember faintly saying, 'Lord, I put up my sail for anything.'

The other memory was of tears springing to my eyes as I watched Rozi and some other small girls singing and doing the actions for a song they had been taught: 'He brought me to his banqueting table and his banner over me is love.'

'Do you really love me, Lord?' I wondered.

Back home again, I idly picked up a torn page from one of the many books that kind friends had given to the children, and read these words:

'Mr Kite, Mr Kite! Why are you lying on the ground?'

'I can't fly till Mr Wind comes and picks me up.'

I had a dream around that time that I was sitting with my knitting and doing children's puzzles on the beach. The tide was coming in slowly. Suddenly a big wave swept me out to sea and I was in a strong current of water. I lost all the little things I had been so busy with. I woke up.

God spoke to me, 'I am going to do that for you.'

We had friends in Kenya who had, as Christians, received the baptism of the Holy Spirit, but I had felt

rather superior to them. I had been brought up in a
Christian home, attended a Christian school and gone
to Bible College. I knew so much! Maybe the baptism
of the Holy Spirit was all right for them, but we didn't
need anything else. But now when Julian suggested
that we go for prayer to a pastor who had received
this gift, I agreed with alacrity.

The pastor had arranged for a babysitter to look after
Pete during our meeting, but the babysitter didn't turn
up, so Pete played with some toys beside us as the
pastor talked to us. And while he prayed for us, Pete
was between us, holding both of our hands.

As a result of that meeting our joy was overwhelming.
Our marriage, which had been a good one, was
suddenly revolutionised with joy. Most of all, we were
overcome with a new love for God and his Word, and
for others.

7

Nursery School and Hospital Hill

I know the plans I have for you, plans for good . . .

Our leave came to an end. We returned to Kenya, leaving Jonathan at school in England – very thankfully, happier; but it was a painful decision. Pete, although rejoicing at being able to run outside without having to wear innumerable woolly clothes, was very unsettled for a time. Every night for three months I had to read or tell him the same story of 'Jon the Shepherd', from the Arch series of children's books. And he was inseparable from me until we returned to a conference at Ashburnham, in Sussex, in August 1975 where, after we had prayed specifically about his fears, he happily joined the 'Fish Club'.

That time we were very sad to have to leave Rozi behind too, in secondary school. It was like a little death each time, leaving the children, or like having an arm cut off, though it was wonderful to be able always to trust the Rock, God himself, to stand with them. But I still wept.

Now we just had Pete at home in Nairobi. We entertained many families from Sudan and northern

31

Kenya at that time, and we had dear American friends living in nearby flats, so Pete was not entirely lonely. But he loved the school holidays when Jonathan and Rozi previously, and now Colin, came back on the St Andrew's bus. Also, Colin had an orthodontic problem, which meant he had to visit a Nairobi dentist quite regularly, so, to Pete's delight, he was often with us at weekends.

But Pete's great pleasure was the twice-termly 'viso', when parents were invited to the school for a concert or sports event. Pete would be lifted out of bed at six o'clock on those Saturday mornings and wrapped in a blanket with his pillow (and, of course, Bun-bun). We would drive in the tropical darkness along roads empty of lorries. Occasionally a giraffe would cross the road ahead of us. We dressed Pete while we stopped to breakfast in the fresh dawn, overlooking the Rift Valley's huge expanses of plain and sky. Our second stop was always at Nakuru for coffee (and proper loos!) before turning off to N'joro along the good new road that wound up the far side of the Rift Valley, passing through large farms, some still European-owned. By the time we had climbed to 7,000 feet, we had our sweaters on. Finally, the road crossed the railway line and approached the school through glorious beds of lilies and blue agapanthus. At the school entrance, black and fair-haired children were waiting in their red and grey uniforms, eagerly looking out for their families.

Pete was taken off with great excitement to be shown round, and we watched sports, swimming or dancing. Lunch was always a family picnic in the forest near the school dam, where the children had us all to themselves. It only ever rained once or twice: visos were usually gloriously sunny days.

It was Pete's isolation from other children – there were none within easy walking distance – that made us decide to send him to nursery school earlier than we had sent the others. There, his humour and creative side showed; every day he brought pictures home. Many were of 'pin men' fighting – he had a passion for soldiers and battles, which was odd considering his gentle nature. Once he brought home a plain green page.

'What's this, Pete?' I asked, as all good nursery school mothers are meant to ask.

'It's gween gwass gwowing,' he told me solemnly.

He came home too with glorious versions of the songs they were being taught. He would collect his entire family together in the holidays and sing them; we struggled to maintain straight faces though we were inwardly bursting with laughter! Jonathan and Rozi had often put on plays in the past, so Pete always enjoyed acting. The drawstring curtains between the dining room and sitting-room came in very handy. His education was proceeding in other ways, too. In our home, the constant coming and going of young Kenyans from the church meant that he grew up without being race-conscious. When he later spent a year at Hospital Hill, a local school, he made many friends. If I foolishly asked him if a particular friend was of Indian, English or brown Kenyan origin, he would look at me perplexed; it was something he never noticed.

Pete really threw his heart into the English Sunday School now. Before the 1975 'Fish Club' experience I have already mentioned, he would only stay in my class, where he found it hard to sit still for long. But now he would happily go to his own class, though usually he was the only pink child in the room.

We returned to England again on leave. This time the Lord provided a house for us in Pembury, Kent.

Pete was very lonely in the village school, where he felt more of an expatriate than he had in Kenya. The other children were not sure about him either. One boy, puzzled at Pete's accent, asked him, 'Are you a white Indian?'

But he did enjoy climbing through our hedge and playing 'soldiers' with the two small boys next door. He also enjoyed visiting Colin and Rozi at their respective secondary schools, as Colin was by now also attending an English boarding school.

Two years previously, Julian's mother had died, bequeathing to us her flat in Folkestone. During this visit we felt we should sell it and look for a permanent base in England, for the sake of our three children whom we were now leaving behind. After much prayer, the Lord directed us to this house between Rozi and Colin's schools – another miracle. One might say that Pete was brought up in an atmosphere of the miraculous. The house had been built in an ancient orchard; Pete suggested we called it 'Apple Garden'. We finally chose 'Applewood'.

Pete and I spent much time together, for Julian was speaking for the mission in many churches. We visited Rozi and Colin's school chapels quite often on Sundays. Colin's was best – it had high pews, Pete could read or colour easily out of sight.

Jonathan was now at the South Bank Polytechnic in London, working hard and busy with the Christian Union. During his last year at school he had been walking in Tunbridge Wells, praying, and very puzzled as to what God wanted him to do, especially as we were so far away. He glanced up and saw 'Careers Office' above a door, so he walked in. A secretary was laboriously telling him that he would have to wait weeks for an interview, when a man walked through the room. He stopped and asked, 'Can I help you, sonny?' He was the top officer and gave Jonathan an hour of his time! He suggested that with all Jonathan's varied interests his best option was to do a degree in Building Administration at South Bank, which would be far more use to him than a university degree in geology.

It was so good having him come to visit us regularly at weekends in his ancient Mini! He was always the life and soul of the party.

Once, when visiting the Ashburnham Christian Conference Centre, Pete and I were exploring. I stopped to talk to one of the men who were working on a prayer centre there. They had renewed the fountain in the middle of the old stable yard as a symbol of the Holy Spirit. I listened intently to what he was saying, but occasionally turned, as mothers do, to see what Pete was doing.

'Excuse me!' I suddenly said. And ran.

Pete had slipped and fallen right into the fountain pool. It was a very narrow gap – hardly eighteen inches – and he could easily have banged his head, but he was only wet through. I was rather awed as I half carried the soaking lad back to our room. Had he been baptised into something special?

8

Returning with Pete from England: Turi

The three of us returned to Nairobi. It was awful leaving Jonathan, Rozi and Colin behind, but there was little time to think at Heathrow airport as we boarded a very ancient plane that seemed to have a miscellany of seats taken from all sorts of charter planes that we had previously flown in. The taps in the basins worked, but they were all dirty and the cupboards were broken. We decided that though it was very cheap, we would never fly with that airline again! I don't know what Pete thought about it all, but he was immensely looking forward to being home again, seeing Nicky, our dog, and leaving the cold weather behind. (In preparing the house in England for tenants, our personal property had had to be stored in the garage. We had to carry it there on a sledge because of the deep snow in Kent!)

We were lovingly welcomed back by our church and many other friends. They had arranged a welcome party that afternoon. The following day we went to the wedding of some dear friends, but tiredness made us reluctantly leave the reception (held in the cathedral hall) before the end. Pete was only too glad to continue unpacking toys left behind sixteen months earlier, and to romp round the garden with the dog.

On Sunday we went to Ziwani again. Pete, greatly enjoying being back with his friends, was becoming used to being a child of two continents. After lunch he was again absorbed in his 'second Christmas' – unpacking, with exclamations of delight, all the toys that had been stored away. He was especially glad to see his large collection of Lego, which had benefited from hand-downs from the other three children. And there were toys to be unpacked that we'd brought back from England: the new sets of soldiers, paints for painting them the correct colours and also a whole selection of dinosaurs, all lovingly bought with his pocket money. (Later, it was several years before I could walk past the model shop in Camden Road, Tunbridge Wells without pain.)

Suddenly on that Sunday, a great fear of losing him came over me. He was an apparently happy, placid child who I knew was very gentle and sensitive. He was just 9 years old, and he found sleeping in strange places difficult. Why in the world were we going to send him to boarding school at St Andrew's, Turi, when there were several good English-syllabus day schools in Nairobi? (The reasons, in fact, had been: it had to be an English-syllabus school because of the requirements of secondary and tertiary education in England. The other three children had implored us to send him to Turi where they had been so happy; and it was the only Christian school. But it was oh, so far away!) When Pete had gone back to playing, after lunch, I began to pour it all out to Julian.

'We prayed about coming back to Kenya – but have we really prayed about sending Pete to boarding school? He's such a sensitive little chap. I'm really worried that we are doing the wrong thing.' It was one week until the start of term.

Julian said cheerfully, 'Well, let's go and pray about it now. But I think it's right.'

We left the plates on the table, went to our spare room and cried out to the Lord.

'We don't even know if Turi is still a good Christian school,' I said. 'We've been away for four terms. It may be awful now.'

I wept, 'Lord, I'm so confused. Please show us your plan for Pete. Please let us know if Turi is any good as a Christian school or even academically now and show us for certain it's your place for Pete.'

The doorbell rang. Julian went to see who was there and I washed my face. It was Peter and Ann Kanyi with flowers and fruit to welcome us back. Rather shamefacedly I cleared the table and prepared tea. We spent a happy few hours with them, then Julian said he would drive them back, in our borrowed car, to their house. I had the kind of headachy feeling one has after weeping a lot. Nicky the dog was whining and jumping around, demanding a walk. I said to Pete, 'Let's take him down to the river.'

We walked down the old cobbled and gravelled road outside our house to the muddy Nairobi River, where we had often played 'Pooh-sticks' on the little footbridge. We decided to return home in case Julian came back and found the house locked. As we turned back, a car was making its way down over the runnels and loosened rocks caused by the November rain. We grabbed Nicky (who was stupid with cars), and I walked on head down. A cheerful voice hailed us from the car.

'Hello! Great to see you back!'

It was our new neighbours, Roger and Jill, and their family.

As we chatted I asked about where they had been. 'Was the Brackenhurst conference good?'

'We didn't go to the conference this year. We've just had a wonderful few days' holiday up at Turi, staying with two Christian teachers. It really is an outstanding school. I'm sure it's the best school in the country!'

I don't know if my mouth fell open, but I do know that I thanked them but did not tell them about my prayer. I walked back on light feet up the hill, with an awed sense of the Lord's loving care for us and for Pete. I spent the next few days sorting out old Turi uniforms and sewing on the necessary name-tapes, but I now did it with a peaceful heart. Pete, although a little apprehensive, was quite excited at the prospect of going to Turi. He was not really a new boy, for he had been going up there ever since he was two months old!

When we finally arrived at the start of term I explained to his Kenyan matron that he needed aspirin to help him to sleep if he was overexcited. She nodded, smiling in the way that teachers, matrons and nurses smile when they think they are dealing with an overanxious mother. I prayed, 'Don't let me be like that, Lord.' But all the while I knew in my heart that this school was the right place for Pete, and that the Lord would take care of things for him: he was his child. We were introduced to Toby, a classmate, who was to look after Pete for the first few days. At first Pete was rather put out by this, for he already knew Turi well. But in his gentle way he accepted the situation.

'Bye, Mum. Bye, Dad.' He hugged us and ran off to supper with Toby.

It was the end of an era.

9

Turi Years

A week later, we rather fearfully opened his first letter home.

Dear Mum and Dad,
  It's good fun up here in Turi. We're going to learn about the North and South Pole. I got to sleep very late last night. I sit on the same table as Toby in class. I have a pencil and ruler of my own. I unpacked my trunk this morning. I have joined Nature. Please keep all the stamps and leave them on the envelopes please.

Love from
Pete

His teacher added a note: 'Peter has settled down very quickly into the school routine. He is terribly happy and really enjoys his work and play.'

This made us rejoice and marvel, though I still felt he was putting on a brave face. Then came his first Visiting Day. Instead of the thin, sad, pinched little chap his mother expected, we were greeted by a cheerful person wearing a red sweater,

'Hello Mum and Dad! Super to see you. Yes, we have got a hockey match later. Yes, I'm very well. Um – excuse me, but I've just got to go and play with Marky-Ann. See you soon.' And he was off!

We stood and looked at each other, then roared with laughter. We parked the car and walked down to the field to meet the great Marky-Ann, not sure whether we were going to meet a boy or a girl. We discovered a shock-headed, cheerful Dutch boy, who had actually been christened Mark Jan!

Pete's second letter read, '*I'm having a nice time here. But I can't get to sleep yet.*' I tried to talk to the matron again, but I knew Pete never fussed, so unless she actually went into his room and saw that he was still awake, she would not know about the problem. But Pete made the best of a bad job. He took to having great games in the toilet section at night with a few friends, climbing over the walls and swinging on bars.

He must have been caught sometimes. His first term dormitory report said, 'He has settled in very well, makes his bed, is very helpful and very cheerful. A lovely boy.' It changed in the second term to, 'Peter, this term, has been rather naughty and not so helpful. He is tidy and clean and always very pleasant.' I think most of us who knew him could easily imagine him there, with his innocent-looking eyes full of mischief, but we were surprised to learn he was tidy!

His headmaster later wrote:

He had such a lovely open character, with a zest for life and willingness to 'have a go' at anything. He won so many friends by being a friend and was unusually sensitive to other people's needs at that young age. There was a radiance about him – surely the radiance of Jesus – which was very winning. He was also great fun, always up to playful tricks and full of good humour.

A friend of Pete's remembers the fun that four of them had with an old broken Land Rover, in which they played, imagining great safaris. Pete used to sit 'on the roof, keeping a look out "for leo-pards" (as he called them) and ducking low-hanging branches as we hurtled down our imaginary road'. Then they would dive into a pile of old thatch from the pavilion roof that was being mended, and tunnel dens and passages into it. 'I can't remember how many hours we spent in "our world" . . . but this is how I remember Pete – grinning, red hair stuck with bits of straw.'

Years later, when asked to write about his spiritual development Pete wrote:

My parents are dedicated missionaries, who really love the Lord. I have then, been brought up always believing in Jesus, God and the Holy Spirit.

There was a long period between the ages of 7 and 12 years old when I often asked Jesus into my heart, but, expecting some dramatic change to occur, was not sure where I stood. However on 1st January 1984 after listening to my father and sister talking about becoming a Christian, I asked for the last time, and since then have always claimed, if only to myself, that I am a Christian.

I remember one of those times. He had gone to bed, when a worried face reappeared round the door. 'Mum,' he said urgently, 'I need you badly.' Puzzled, I followed him; he climbed under a blanket on his top bunk, turned to me with tears in his eyes and said 'Mum, how can I be sure I'm a Christian?' I took him to God's word which says 'Look! I stand at the door

and knock: if anyone hears my voice and opens the
door, I will come into his house and eat with him.'
'That's what God says Pete and he will never break his
word. If you ask him he will come into your heart and
cleanse you from all your mistakes and give you power
for every day and most amazingly be your friend. This
makes you God's son, the most incredible relationship
in the world' (Revelation 3:20). This verse is heavily
underlined in his Good News Bible, but I think that
the time he mentions was when he was all by
himself.

To Pete's sorrow, Marky-Ann left with his parents
when their contract ended. But he soon made two other
great friends: one, the son of a Ugandan ambassador
and the other, the son of a racing driver. Neither were
active Christians, but Pete faithfully chugged along to
the Scripture Union meetings every Sunday afternoon.
He flung himself into Scouts and the school clubs, and
also into his own 'Secret Club', which involved creeping
around, hidden from sight from the staff. He did well
in sport, and was eventually a member of the rugby
and cricket first teams, and he did moderately well in
his work; but his friends were his great interest.

However, in spite of the fun he had at school, his
greatest joy was the holidays when we would go to the
airport to collect his brothers and sister from England,
coming back, usually in the dawn, opening the white
gates and hooting as we came down the drive so that
anyone else would rush out to greet the travellers.

During most of the holidays we managed to take the
children away for at least a few days, sometimes going
north to stay with other missionaries or travelling to
one of the game parks that had self-catering *bandas*
(small two-roomed stone huts, which provided the
basic necessities of life).

Twice we went to the fabled Island Camp. The Rift Valley appears at its deepest in Kenya where the Kenyan highlands soar on either side to seven or eight thousand feet. There are many hollows that form lakes in this amazing crack in the earth's surface. Just north of the Equator is one of the most beautiful. Its name is Lake Baringo, and it is flanked on the north side by the blue hills of Pokot. When Pete was 4 years old, Jonathan had persuaded his geography teacher to come out to Kenya for the summer holidays to tour the remarkable geological formations all over Kenya. It was they who discovered for us a beautiful island in this lake, a portion of which had been made a camping place. As residents of Kenya and Turi parents, we were entitled to special concessions there at that time.

The owners had bought a small rocky area from the Njemps (the inhabitants of the island) and had set up permanent tents on cement floors. When we visited it, Pete slept on a camp bed between ours. I remember I watched his every move during the day after various members of the family had seen five snakes among the rocks. The open-sided dining room overlooking the lake was visited by many brilliantly coloured birds; and to the children, perhaps especially Pete, it was the epitome of Kenyan fun.

There were other favourite places, for example a cottage called 'Trees', high up on the escarpment below the Aberdare range, which was a favourite bolthole for us. But the August holiday each year always saw us return to Mombasa.

As missionaries we were not rich in the sense that most people would think of riches. But few of Pete's wealthy school friends could have had such holidays. Take Mombasa. Mombasa is a general name not only for the city but also for the whole stretch of Kenya's comparatively short coastline. On those almost snow-white beaches were hotels and also many small stone bungalows built by far-sighted residents during the previous eighty years or so. We used to rent a bungalow for ten days on the south coast, on Diani or Tiwi beach, which was about seventeen miles down rather poor roads from Mombasa town. It was much cheaper than a hotel. In the early days, we had to fetch most of our supplies from Mombasa, but now there are small *dukas* (small shops originally run by Indians, but now mostly by Kenyans) springing up all along the coast.

Arriving and seeing that great shore was always breathtaking. After leaving the Nairobi highlands and driving for mile after mile through grey-green scrub on the coastal plain, suddenly one rounded a bend in the road, and there was the sea. It truly is a coastal paradise: the beach, edged with coconut palms; the white sand with small bands of black seaweed; the great lagoon of shifting blue and green light, edged on the horizon with the white waves breaking on the dark coral reef.

The first thing Julian did when we arrived (if the car had not had serious problems on the way, meaning our holiday would be dominated by garages) was to locate the tide tables and calculate which would be the best day to find a fisherman to take us out to the reef. That was always a special day. We marvelled at a whole series of God-made miniature caves and rock pools, filled with curious creatures and unbelievably fast, brilliant-coloured fish. When we put on goggles and submerged our heads underwater it was like C.S. Lewis's tales of Narnia: we were transported into a new world of glorious different coloured corals and other sea plants, in which lived the myriad varieties of brilliant fish. We had to be careful, though, to avoid sunburn on the backs of our legs while goggling lying on inflated inner tubes (or bending over rock pools), and lion fish or stonefish lurking in the rocks – accidentally touching one could mean paralysis or even death. But the beauty of the reef was awe-inspiring.

It was wonderful to have time together as a family. In Nairobi, Julian was out a great deal; if he was not in the office, he was at a committee meeting. I had become very involved with refugees who, in theory, were living and working in Nairobi, but usually were unemployed and desperate for help, advice and hope. Our house, too, was full of other visitors, which we loved. But in spite of cancelling many of the church week-day meetings, like women's meetings, during school holidays, we had little time alone with the children. However, I did try to make time to read to them, even when visitors were around. We enjoyed Arthur Ransome, John Buchan, C.S. Lewis, R.L. Stevenson and many others. One friend recounts, 'I seem to remember it was *The Last Battle* (C.S. Lewis), and seeing you together, and the complete concentration and absorption on Pete's face as he listened, snuggling against you, said such a lot.'

We were doing a four-year stint before going on to another 'home assignment', partly because of Pete's school terms. We had once muddled Jonathan's schooling and, though he did catch up very well afterwards, we did not want to make the same mistake again. However, we returned to England in July 1984 for a few very happy weeks for Jonathan's wedding to Sharon, a lovely nurse whom he had met the year before. We met her for the first time only a week before the wedding, but we were delighted with the person God had given him. We were glad, too, to see the flat that he had been able to buy and to hear of all their plans for decorating it. He had now finished his studies and gone into a good job as a project officer.

We stayed with my sister, as we had rented Applewood out to tenants. Pete had been glad to escape from school a week early, but Rozi, Colin and he could not wait to get back to Kenya and have their holiday at the coast as usual – though it would be strange this year without Jonathan.

Pete was to have very long holidays that year! On our way back from Mombasa he developed a swollen gland. It turned out to be mumps. He was just about to start his final year at Turi, but there was no way that the matron would permit a child to return who was still infectious. So that year Pete's holiday was extended for three weeks. It was special, too, because Colin had just finished at Tonbridge School and was starting his 'gap year' between school and university; and Rozi did not have to return till October for her work. So the three of them accompanied us to one of Julian's yearly major activities, the organisation of the orientation of all new missionaries who had arrived within the last twelve months.

Rozi did a brilliant job of organising the sleeping arrangements for sixty people, and Colin joined the volunteers in their dormitory, as that year he was to be a volunteer himself (he had plans to go and help with a reforestation project). Pete, in a kind of quarantine, slept with us in a cottage and had great fun with his brother and sister in the beautiful highland resort where the orientation was held. He also did some work for his Common Entrance exam, which he was to sit the following June.

Orientation week ended, Rozi returned to college and we took Pete (now a prefect) back to Turi.

Colin's plans, however, fell through. News came that the parents of the missionaries with whom he was to stay had been badly hurt in an accident, so he stayed on with us well into October. He helped with the refugees and drove the car around for us, as he had just passed his Kenyan driving test, but still felt rather in limbo. One day, feeling very concerned for him, Julian 'happened' to be going to Mayfield, our mission guesthouse. He saw Art and Mary Ellen Davis there.

'Art, would it be possible for you to take a volunteer to help with your building project in Orus, for a few weeks?'

Art cheerfully agreed, and even asked if Colin would drive one of his vehicles up for him, to take an experienced well-digger up to the site.

'Have you ever been up that way, Julian?' Art asked. 'You should come and visit us.'

'I used to visit a school up in Kinyang, when I was doing school supervision before we were married,' replied Julian, 'but I've never been up your side, towards Churo. What's the road like now? I went up in my ancient Land Rover; the road was washed out in one place, I remember, so I had to make a big detour. It was so hot you didn't feel like talking to anybody. It was just dry, hot rock.'

'The road's not bad through Tangulbei and Churo now,' Art reassured him. 'That really helped us when we lived in Amaya – but now that we are camping in Orus, it's still fun in the mud up our road when it rains!'

Long before, my brother-in-law – an eye surgeon – had travelled round running clinics amongst the Tugen. He had told us about the occasional Pokot he had seen. A friend of his, travelling home on a cargo boat, had enthralled a young Englishman called Tom Collins with his stories of these people. Tom felt so certain that he should go to preach to them that, in spite of being turned down by the mission board in London on account of his very weak heart, he sold his possessions, bought a boat ticket for Mombasa and rode his motor cycle along 300 miles of dirt roads to Nairobi. For twenty-five years he wandered with the Pokot families, as they looked for food and water for their herds. They listened to him and he helped translate the New Testament for them, but when he was dying he reckoned that he had only seen two really turn to the Lord.

After a dry year when many cattle died, some Pokot started to take up agriculture near the centre called Churo. A new all-weather road of muram (gravel) went through Churo to take tourists up to the northern deserts. Kenyan Christians in Nakuru sent Kenyan missionaries to work there, and led some Pokot to Jesus. Another missionary, travelling through from the north, found a man in Churo who was very ill with ulcers. He took him to a mission hospital near Nairobi, where he was not only healed but came to faith in Jesus. When he returned to Churo, Pastor Samuel, the Kenyan missionary, encouraged him; and when later, Art and Mary Ellen came to work there, he was their right-hand man.

His name was Reuben.

'But, Art,' asked Julian, 'why have you moved to Orus? Did I hear that the church leaders from the area asked you to?'

'Yes, they did. Although some Pokot have begun to settle and farm around Churo, there are still many who just herd their cows and goats in the traditional way. These are usually around Orus. In the rainy season when the grass grows high it is excellent for cattle.'

So, one year before this meeting between Julian and Art, Art and Mary Ellen (and their three children, in the holidays) *had travelled up over the rocks in an ancient vehicle to live in tents in Orus. Reuben and his wife and cows went with them. It was very brave of Reuben, for his fellow tribespeople were very angry about his decision to become a Christian, and he had left his farm in Churo. Also, there were many wild animals in Orus at that time. One night, Reuben had had to chase lions away from his cows.*

'The trouble is,' explained Art, 'there's no permanent water there. That is what we are trying to help with. If there were water, the herds could stay, the people would settle and they could have more continuous teaching.'

'So is that why you want Colin to bring up the well-digger *fundi* [somebody who is an expert in his or her field]?'

'Yes – we've just been told by an expert that there is underground water there and we hope eventually to get another organisation to help us put in a dam for the cattle. At present we have to fill up 100-gallon water drums in Tangulbei. When can Colin come? We'd like to go this week.'

Colin was delighted. He not only helped them put up some cement-based metal *rondavel* huts, but he also later installed the plumbing for the little two-roomed house that the Davises had built.

That was how our involvement with the Pokot people began.

Pete, meanwhile, was in his last year at Turi. Having started it as a prefect, in the second term he was made Head Boy, so now he had to tow the line! But he had a great sympathy for those who were 'having fun', and was much loved. His cousin Ruth wrote:

Pete always seemed to bring humour into every situation. The amazing thing was that his 'fun' was just that. It never went too far or became destructive but was warm and comfortable. He was never into cliques, but managed to include whoever he could. I know he made my stay at Turi far less intimidating.

One of his last letters from Turi shows how, even then, he would hold no bitterness in his heart.

Hiya Mum and Dad,
How's it? I'm fine up here, yeah! Great! Well there's heaps of news.

Well CE [Common Entrance – an examination to a secondary private school in England] went fine, lovely papers, all reasonably easy and I enjoyed it much more than going to lessons, and, as I said the papers were quite easy. Well, they're over so school's GREAT.

Yesterday we played Pembroke [Pete was now in the First 15 for rugby]. Fabulous game, I really enjoyed it, but we lost it. I sort of scored. I mean it was a try but the ref. said it was a Pem. bloke who touched it down, must admit he couldn't see. Then one of their tries was a chap who had been tackled and on the floor he picked the ball up and dumped it on the other side, then as one of us kicked the ball it went into the others' half. He knocked it on over the line then dived at it, worst luck, and the ref. counted it, ugh! Oh well, too bad.

Pete finished in July 1985. We collected the last Turi school trunk after seventeen years. We said all our goodbyes. Then came another dash to the airport, and soon we were in England, rejoicing at having the children together once again at Applewood.

10

To Tonbridge

The summer holidays quickly came to an end. It was a
bewildering time for me. We were back in Applewood,
suitcases unpacked, all my brood in the same country,
and I suppose I thought that everything would be just
like last time. But when we suggested family outings,
they looked at me confused.

'Oh! Sorry Mum. I've something else arranged.'

Julian was much quicker than I was to realise that
Rozi and Colin were virtually grown up, like Jonathan.
At least I still had one child to look after! Julian saw
that an ordinary family holiday by the sea was out
that year, but knowing how disappointed Pete would
be, we arranged for him to go to Cornwall with his
cousins, who had been at Turi with him.

Jonathan and Sharon, Rozi and Colin came home
quite often. Pete loved having them around, but, as
usual, found plenty to do when they were away:
making models, walking round the countryside with
Julian, and the immense pleasure of sorting out the
little bedroom that had been Colin's on our previous
leave (Colin was now upgraded to Jonathan's room), as
well as kindly helping generally in house and garden. I

sorted out our belongings that had been mothballed for four years – 'the Jacksons' perfume', our sister-in-law laughingly called it – and organised clothes for Pete's new school.

Tonbridge School is a boarding public school in the castle town of Tonbridge, eight miles from Applewood. Pete knew it fairly well from his many visits to Colin. We fished out the Jonathan/Colin trunk and the Jonathan/Colin tuck box. Pete was too laid-back to bother to put his name on them; he enjoyed being his brothers' brother. In many ways he was looking forward to following in Colin's footsteps, but we all felt apprehensive as we parked our red Nova beside the Mercedes in the drive of Judde House[4] and walked up to the housemaster's front door for the Novaes' (the Tonbridge term for new boys) parents' tea, the day before the rest of the school arrived. Mr and Mrs Pendered welcomed us very kindly, as usual. We were introduced to several boys and their parents in the lovely drawing room, balancing cups of tea and trying to look at ease. Someone helped Pete hump his trunk upstairs to the dormitory, where he chose a bed near the door (warmer for the winter). He later moved, to sleep by the window, as he found it was easier to read his Bible in the morning while the others were still asleep.

Karl St Hilaire, another new boy, writing about that day and his first meeting with Pete, said:

> I left the welcoming party and proceeded to explore my limited boundaries. It was not long before I noticed a young lad pursuing my tail. He had a bowl of blonde hair on his head and was no taller than me.
>
> 'Why are you following me?' I asked. He looked startled.
>
> 'Oh, I don't know. Something to do until the rest of them get here, I guess. My name is Rupert, what's yours?'

I hesitated. 'Rupert? What sort of name is that?'

'It's a good English name, that's what it is!' he replied angrily. I could tell I was not the first person to question his name.

I apologised and defended my ignorance, 'I'm sorry. I'm not accustomed to English heritage yet . . . I'm from Canada. . . .'

That night I was introduced to one who would later become the third of our trio – Pete. He slept in the bed next to Rupert, and they found they had much in common. Pete, too, was in the school choir [just as Colin had been]. He came across as a square-headed, goody-two-shoes who had never done an egregious thing in his life. Coincidentally, he, too, was my height. He had red hair with the traditional freckles, and had an unfortunate lisp with his letter 'R'. Now, under normal circumstances a lisp is nothing to be ashamed of. However, in a boarding school where first impressions determined your fate amongst the seniors, I could tell that Pete would be at their mercy. So for the following two weeks Rupert and I, with a little help from Big Bird, taught him the secrets behind producing the letter 'R'.

During that time, we lost our instinctive pretences, and I realised that first impressions were not a good basis for judgement. Pete's father was a missionary and like father like son, he, too, was a firm believer. I had nothing against that fact, but I was concerned that religion would decollate our friendship. However, Pete was not as possessive as others were on this topic, and my hesitation quickly dissolved. In fact, he is responsible for the little faith I have today. He was born in Kenya, and though he liked to make us believe he was Kenyan, he did not have the sun tolerance nor the passport to make his story convincing. However, the fact that he had lived off the island, gave us something to build our friendship on. His dreams led him back to his homeland, Kenya, to work in the outback with the tribes he admired. Pete's charisma became the glue that kept our trio together and, before long, we were inseparable friends.

Colin, remembering the struggles he'd had as a new boy at that school, had not been unmindful of his little brother either. I remember him spending a long, late evening giving Pete the lowdown on how to stand one's ground and survive. Both his brothers and sister kept ringing us to hear how he was getting on. Colin was very pleased to hear from one of the senior boys that Pete had been found at the top of the circular staircase in the House, dropping marbles over the banisters.

'What on earth do you think you are doing, child!' he was angrily asked, by a hot and bothered prefect running up the stairs.

'Oh I just wanted to see if they would go to the bottom,' Pete innocently replied.

We soon started travelling around the country for AIM, taking meetings in churches and for students. But we called in to visit Pete as often as we could, and were kindly allowed to keep all exeats (free weekends) and half-terms free. I missed him sorely. As we tried to keep house and garden under control as well as writing and travelling, I have forgotten much of that autumn, but I do remember some outstanding incidents. I remember Julian searching all the local advertising papers that were shoved through our front door to find a reasonably-priced mini billiards table, so that when it was too cold he and Pete could have something to do together. It gave Pete hours of fun.

I remember Julian's 60th birthday. We arranged two things: a party at home for family and friends, and a trip to a concert at the Royal Festival Hall in London, for which Jonathan generously bought tickets.

Mr Pendered allowed Pete an extra exeat. We had to wait until a sports match was over, and we picked him up in school clothes. Then we navigated the maze of London streets to meet Jonathan and Sharon at their flat – I remember it was the first time I had ever seen people sleeping on London pavements.

Jonathan had got us excellent seats about halfway up the auditorium. Rozi met us in the foyer, but Colin had not yet arrived. We were not allowed to wait for him; like most concert halls, they were very insistent on the audience being seated at the right time. I pleaded with the usher to let Colin creep in late – he was coming from Southampton University, where he was now a student, and the only train he could get after his lectures gave him very little time to get to the concert hall. The man said he would do his best. While the orchestra tuned up, we anxiously watched the door. Suddenly we saw Colin's yellow head, and the usher bowing him in. What a boy! In some ancient trousers, Kenyan safari boots and a good old *kikoi* (a Kenyan striped cloth worn by men at the coast, popular with tourists) wound round his neck, plus of course an armful of raincoats, he mounted the stairs, a big smile on his face. There was almost a cheer from the Jackson row. We all hugged him and settled down for a wonderful evening. Later, as we were leaving, a Canadian who had been sitting in front of us said to me,

'What a wonderful family you have! I enjoyed them far more than the concert!'

I remember, too, my immense disappointment, another small 'dying' inside me, when I missed hearing Pete sing in the end of term carol service, because of an important engagement at Cambridge.

I remember Christmas, and the thrill of having all the family with us. That year we had invited the local dustbin man and his wife to join us. On Boxing Day, we had a wonderful walk in crisp, frost-covered countryside, all dressed up snugly in weird and wonderful woolly coats, scarves, gloves and boots; and I remember the sadness, after all the laughter and games we played along the way, of finding a bird hanging upside down with its claw caught between twigs. Although Colin, our bird expert, held it very gently and released its foot, sadly it died of exhaustion in his hand.

11

Easter Holidays

When the Easter holidays came, we were in Scotland for meetings, so Colin and Pete joined us. Neither had been to Scotland before. Pete's prejudiced comment was, 'Well, I see there are some good places in Britain.'

A few days later we packed into the Nova again and headed off to Minehead for our first Spring Harvest conference.[5] It was a long journey. Colin did most of the driving, but we were all glad to get a break at my brother Richard's thirteenth-century vicarage in Congresbury, which was on our way. It was good, too, for Pete to contact his cousins again; he had not met them for several years. In fact I think he was sad to leave them, and all our hearts sank a little as we joined the huge queue of cars wending their way through Devon roads in the pouring rain. Our hearts sank further when we found that we would not be allowed to park our car by the chalet we had been allocated. But we cheered up when we eventually got the keys to turn in the lock and saw inside it – two bedrooms, a good living room and a TV! The family had jointly decided that we should not have a TV at home, as the children were all studying, so to have one on holiday was special.

Pete was a little sceptical of it all. I well remember his look of dismay as he opened the huge pack of literature we had received at the gate.

'Oh Mum, Dad, this is going to be foul. They have groups for babies and toddlers, and then one for 12–14-year-olds. A programme for 12-year-olds will be so boring, just babyish!' proclaimed Pete, who had turned 14 before Christmas.

I knew Pete was very enduring and would put up with a lot without grumbling, but I was distressed to think of him having an entire dismal week. I mumbled something about being sure he could come to the adult meetings if he wished.

But Colin spoke up. 'Pete, you just try it. Maybe it will be better than you think. You needn't go again if you find it's boring.'

Accommodating as ever, he went off with his brother to find the dance hall (Spring Harvest is held in seaside holiday camps) where his group was to meet. When we all returned for lunch, Pete was beaming.

'It was brilliant, Mum and Dad. They have us all in gangs and I'm in the Mau Mau. We've got to dress up tomorrow. I'll have to get some hair gel.'

I had brought some green cake colouring. Between us we made his red hair look amazing.

I had never seen him so keen to get anywhere. He would rush his meals and say, 'I must go. I can't be late!'

Later he came in with awe in his green eyes. 'Mum, it was so wonderful today. We prayed in groups for people who had headaches and were ill and we saw people get better.'

I wanted to hear more about it from him but he was reticent on the subject. But when writing to Youth With A Mission later, he wrote of how that conference changed his life.

In 1986 I attended Spring Harvest with my family. Needless to say that was a great blessing. I'm sure that it was there that I received the Holy Spirit, in a time of just crying.

12

Summer in England

That summer term, Pete began to keep a journal. He
wrote about the Christian Fellowship that he attended
and to which he tried to take some of his friends:
he wrote that it was 'not fantastic'. He wrote, too, a
description of his 'field day' when his party missed the
instructions and got thoroughly lost. It was difficult
asking the way, as Pete had insisted that they should all
dress up 'in combat gear': elderly clothes, a *kikoi* round
his head and swimming goggles 'for protection from
the hail'. One of his friends wouldn't dress up and was
embarrassed because the others were not 'normal'. Pete
wrote, 'I couldn't believe it – he cheered up when
I started a mud fight.' Otherwise, apart from his
exeats, Pete found things were dull at school.

Julian and I were due to return to Kenya in September.
That summer, Jonathan and Sharon had planned a
wonderful trip for us all up Scotland's Caledonian
Canal on a launch. They had been on a launch on Loch
Lomond for their honeymoon and wanted us to have
the same fun. The boat company gave us an instruction
book. It said, 'Choose someone as Captain, someone as

Mate, etc.' The Jacksons, being different, ended up with six Captains and one Ship's Boy!

The big question, though, was how soon everyone could go windsurfing. Unfortunately, a vital part of the sailboard's mast had been left on a beach on the south coast, so at every major town on our way up through England and Scotland we had had to stop to enquire if the missing bit was available. Arriving at last at the water sports centre where our trip was to begin, our hopes were dashed again.

'The place to get it would be Inverness, for sure, sir,' Colin was told.

So that was where everyone wanted to go. In spite of some serious plumbing problems, we had much laughter and some scares, especially getting through locks.

The trip was not without incident either.

The boatman had told us, 'It's very important to put oil into the engine each morning before starting it.' This involved removing a trap door in the floor, approximately 3ft by 1½ft, unscrewing a cap from the tank and filling it up with oil. Easy! Colin kindly offered to be engineer (as well as being one of the captains).

Every morning that the sun was shining we woke up gently rocking on waves glinting with sunshine. Our two birdwatchers/fishermen, Pete and Colin, got into the dinghy and were far away in the rushes while breakfast was being prepared. The drawback in the whole undertaking was the loos, which would not operate for long without the engine being on. One morning, moored in an idyllic bay, disaster struck. The birdwatcher was hastily summoned; the engine was urgently needed. Of course, nothing easier! Cover removed – cap unscrewed and placed carefully on the engine – oil produced!

The next thing we heard was Colin, rather pale-faced, exclaiming 'The cap's gone!'

'What do you mean – gone? It can't have gone!'

'This thing slopes. The boat's rocking. It's down in the sump.'

The underneath of a boat is usually V-shaped; this one was no exception. In this boat, however, under the floorboards not only was there the vast ungainly engine but an entanglement of pipes and wires, mostly covered with cracked silver-coloured padding. And beneath everything else, in the bottom of the 'V', was the inevitable, black, oily sludge. There was no way that any of us except Pete could get in.

'Pete! You'll be a hero!'

'Darling, we hate to ask you . . .'

'Are you sure it's really safe?'

'Do I have to?'

'Whatever else can we do? We're out of radio contact. Another boat may not come by for ages, and we'll never get to Inverness.'

Pete resignedly got into his swimming gear. Urged on with many words of encouragement and six lots of instructions, he wormed his way into the depths and reluctantly put his arm in, elbow-deep in the dank and foul-smelling murk.

But he got the cap, and received VIP treatment on his return – for a while.

When, to our relief, we chugged into the wide stretches of Loch Ness, having eased our way through the many locks, someone gave Pete the steering wheel. I was busy in the cabin.

Suddenly the internal radio crackled into life.

'Calling Silver Spirit, calling Silver Spirit.'

'That's us,' I thought. The strange thing was that we were out of range of radio control with the base. Then

I realised that the message was coming from another boat on the loch.

'Silver Spirit, are you all right?'

'I think so.'

'You seem to be going round in circles,' said the concerned radio voice.

'How kind! Yes – yes, we're OK; thank you for your kindness. Goodbye!'

I called up to the bridge. 'Pete! What are you doing!'

'I was just doing some circles for fun,' said a cheerful voice from the upper deck.

Pete wrote about the holiday in his journal:

> I finished off my Grand Prix car and started my Tank World. I spent 10 days in Scotland going up and down the Caledonian Canal with family. Colin hooked 2 pike, caught 1 trout at Inverness. It was a good time. Saw golden eagle and osprey. Really good fun. I learnt to windsurf on Loch Oich.

He wrote that almost at the end of the holiday. By then we had surmounted many struggles and reached Inverness, where we finally bought the missing part. After many more adventures (including meeting another Peter who was in Pete's form at Tonbridge; he happened to be standing on a lock-side with his mother, as we heaved the huge vessel through), we returned home rather heavy-hearted, to pack up the house ready for tenants. But we were quite sure that we were doing what God wanted us to do. My husband wisely arranged for Pete to stay for part of the time with the aunts, uncles and cousins who would later be his hosts for half-terms, etc.

All too soon we were at Heathrow again, lifting our overweight, elderly suitcases onto the conveyor belt. Our thoughts were full of the family – in particular Sharon, our beautiful daughter-in-law, who had been knocked off her bicycle the day before and had suffered concussion. In the mercy of God she was now so much better that Jonathan was able to be there to see us off. But there was an extra sense of dying this time, as we walked on to the plane by ourselves, leaving all of them behind.

It was no easier just because the three older ones had left school. But when we had asked them what they felt we should do, their reaction was still, 'Stay in Kenya, Dad and Mum. We love coming to visit you there. We'll be all right. We would hate not being able to come to Kenya for the holidays.'

Pete went off in Rozi's car to stay for a few days with my older brother John and his wife Gina in Tunbridge Wells. He knew that a new, more independent, stage of his life had begun. And I do not think he really liked it.

STAGE 2

My fortress . . .
He is my shield and the horn [strength] of my
salvation, my stronghold.
Psalm 18:2

13

Rain and France

Now Pete joined the others in the shuttle service between England and Kenya. He spent that first term by himself trying to find his feet. He was anxious to keep in with his friends and in a sense he kept his Christianity in a separate compartment. He went to the Christian Fellowship most of the time, but his best friends were not members. That term he wrote us many letters, keeping us cheerfully up to date with what was happening – but they always had parts in Swahili and they always complained about the English rain. He kept talking about his great longing to be home again. And he always remembered to send greetings to James, our old cook, and to other Kenyan friends.

There is a picture on the front of one of his airmail letters: a map of England with 'ME' written on it and rain pouring down, then a line to an outline map of Kenya, with a jolly sun shining over it. Half the address and sender's address (from 'Tonbridge Prison School') were washed away, which proved he was right about the rain! It was clever of Kenya Posts and Telecommunications to manage to deliver it.

His letters were also full of the school exchange trip
he was to make to France: 'Oh yes, since I am in
Set 2, I'll be going on an exchange to France and
will be staying with a French family, it would
be great if you could pray for me to get a good
family, otherwise it might be awful.'

The French boy turned out to be 'a really nice guy'.
He visited England first and stayed at the school.
However, the weekend was a problem: all the other
boys were taking their 'guests' home. The school
suggested that Pete should take him to watch a hockey
match but, firstly, it was pouring with English rain,
secondly, the boy had never played hockey and was
not too interested, and thirdly, £8 was to be added to
our termly bill for taking him. 'I was pretty annoyed
at that,' wrote Pete.

When Pete 'just by chance mentioned it to Qureish
Vanat [an Indian friend], he very kindly invited us
to his house for the night in Southend'.

Pete was overwhelmed, too, by the generosity of the
French family when he visited them in France. They
took him to the shops, down the Rhone, up the Eiffel
Tower and much more. He was amazed at the French
diet. 'Instead of cornflakes, we had a bowl of tea
or chocolate with everyone in their PJs.' And his
French improved!

His brothers and sister and loving aunts and uncles
looked after him during his exeats, but even school
was a more cheerful place now he was in his second
year. There were new opportunities and challenges.
For example, having had his appetite whetted on Loch
Oich with windsurfing, he decided to join the school
Navy Corps.

14

New Horizons

On Pete's first school holiday back in Kenya, there were just the three of us at home for a few weeks. So one weekend we took him to a fishing camp on Mount Kenya. He went for long walks with his father and mucked about, fishing and damming a stream. I thought he was bored but he later told me how very much he had enjoyed it. At home he had to share us with so many visitors.

Rozi and Colin also came for Christmas, which was the usual busy time, including parties for different groups in the church. Three missionary ladies who had been marooned for Christmas came to us for meals. Lois Clarke especially remembers Pete – he changed her name to Robert Louis Stevenson, or Roberto for short! He also dressed up as Father Christmas to give out the presents, with gales of laughter as usual.

For the New Year we got away to Trees. It was the last time we would be able to go, for the owners were selling it. Rozi, Colin and Pete saw the New Year in watching the moon over the Rift Valley and the lights of Naivasha twinkling in the valley below. On New Year's Day Colin was unwell but Rozi and Pete went 'bundu bashing' (exploring the bush off the beaten track) on the steep escarpment in front of the house.

It was now Pete's turn to be taught to drive by his father. The gravel farm roads were an ideal place to start.

'Slow down here and turn left at the T-junction, Pete.'

'Help! What's happening?' I yelled from the back, as we lurched onto the grass on the far side of the road, squeezing in between two posts!

'Oh, I suppose I put my foot on the accelerator by mistake,' said Pete thoughtfully. Everyone started talking at once. 'Can't we get on, Dad? We'll never get there with Pete driving!'

Julian calmly said, 'Just put her in reverse, Pete, gently, and try the left road now.'

Pete moved her gently back and moved off more carefully and confidently for a few miles, before giving up to one of the others.

He was growing up fast and taking on new responsibilities. Returning to England with Colin still not fully recovered, Pete had to cope with all the passports and tickets. It was just as well, because at the Easter holiday, now a confident 15-year-old, he had to fly to Kenya by himself. Jonathan and Rozi were working and Colin had gone to be a volunteer at a Christian field study centre and bird observatory in Portugal for three weeks. Pete loved the freedom of the bungalow, making models and enjoying himself on the piano. He never complained of being bored.

Julian would return from the office at 5.30 for tea and the two of them would go off taking our Labrador, Kenny, for a walk, usually in the Arboretum or the Nairobi University grounds. If there were several of us on a walk, Pete would often hang behind.

'Pete, you OK?'

'Yes, I just like being quiet and looking at the trees and birds,' he would say.

We did get away to Elsamere, the nature reserve on Lake Naivasha for a couple of nights. Pete recorded the visit in his journal: *'We woke up in the middle of one night with a hippo just outside which was funny. Me and Mum climbed to Green Lake Crater the next day – fascinating.'*

Back at school, the summer term was packed with fun – climbing, navy and tennis. He mentioned some significant things in his letters. He had started to go to a young people's group at the local church on Sunday evenings and was getting one of his friends to come to the Christian Fellowship (CF) group at school. He was impressed by hearing Chris Foot and a friend speak to the whole school one morning about Christianity. And at half-term, he and his cousin Philip worked on Philip's remote control cars. Pete did the painting, the detailed work he loved. On one he wrote, 'No guts, no glory.' I think he was fast realising that it was true.

The next summer holidays opened up several new horizons. He stayed for a week with Chris on his family's farm in Molo, a township about eight miles from Turi; he drove to Lodwar in the desert of Turkana in north Kenya with his father, who had business there for the church and where they were nearly washed away by a seasonal river; then he enjoyed ten days with the family in Mombasa again. In between, he was busy in his bedroom, supposedly working on a plane model. He also became very interested in the plight of the refugees that he met daily at home, and helped with their food distribution.

But Pete's most significant trip came after Mombasa.

Colin had decided to work on a project for his Environmental Studies degree, evaluating the impact on vegetation of putting in a dam in a semi-arid area. To do his research he was going for a month to a centre near Orus called Kokwo Toto. Colin had come to love the wild country up there, and Pete was to join him for the first week.

Art Davis drove them up to the centre in his Daihatsu.

Besides the three of them and Mary Ellen, they picked up Art's daughter Karen and her friend from their school at Kijabe before starting their five- to six-hour journey to Pokot country.

First they had to stop at Nakuru and then at Loruk. The latter is a police post on the Tugen–Pokot border, just north of Lake Baringo. A few folk had settled there and a couple of missionaries were living among them. Unlike the now settled Tugen, the Pokot, like their northern neighbours the Turkana, were still on the whole a nomadic people, searching for adequate food and water for their herds. The fierce skirmishes between the Pokot and the Turkana were primarily to gain more cows. The whole of life in that arid part depended on their cattle. Pete wrote:

At Loruk the rain started. There was a beautiful smell of flowers just by the Baringo cliffs. We set off for Orus in the dark. Coming up to the top of a hill, there were three red figures which made me jump. It turned out that they were Pokot warriors worshipping the rain. We didn't stop, as sometimes they are possessed. We drove on and a bat-eared fox dashed across the road ahead of us. At Loruk, Col had picked up the Land Rover and was behind us with the girls. We had to wait for them as the girls needed to go to the choo [toilet]. Going along, some stones which were stuck to the spare tyre fell off onto the roof and were making an awful din, so I hung out of the window, in the pouring rain, knocking them off with a crowbar.

We got to Orus, after Colin had got the Land Rover stuck in the mud and had a puncture.

The rain had made the landscape gloriously green. 'Whatever do people eat round here?' Pete asked Art, thinking of the mile after mile of scrubby bushes.

'Because of famine some have started to plant crops near Churo,' he answered. 'But the tough ones think it's a bit sissy to plant like other tribes. They do eat maize meal though, when they can buy it from one of the *dukas* on the main road. Otherwise they live on milk, wild berries and vegetables when in season, and blood that they extract from the jugular vein of their bulls. They take it so skilfully that it doesn't hurt the animal very much. This is what makes cows so extremely important to these people. If a man doesn't have cows, he cannot get married here either, Pete. You know about the bride price that people in Kenya have to pay to their respective in-laws before they can marry? Well, here they have no other form of income besides their cows and a few goats. When a woman gets married, her father gives her a cow or two that are her very own, and a man will give each son a cow at birth. The Masai, to whom these folk are related, have a proverb: "For one thought for yourself, give a hundred to your cows."'

'So is there much cattle rustling these days?' asked Pete.

'No, not for the last six years. The last time was very scary for the Pokot. The Turkana warriors took many of their cows and people were killed. There used to be an Asian *duka* up on the hill here, but during that fighting, they left. The Turkana didn't touch *wazungu* [white people], they were only after cows. But Pokot did get killed, of course, especially when they went out to save their cattle. It was often after a time of drought, when cattle died, that these incidents occurred. It was so scary that the Pokot didn't return here for six years. We were living over at Amaya then. I suppose it could happen again, but people are beginning to send their children to school and settling.'

Pete was fascinated by the people. Near Orus there were more folk on the road, a few warriors near the tea shop and women with small naked boys driving herds of cows. The warriors were rather like Masai, with just a *shuka* [cloth worn by men] tied over one shoulder or round their waist, but a Masai *shuka* is red and these were black. They had strings of beads round their glistening arms, but most remarkable were the headdresses of blue-painted mud and beautiful feathers. They each carried a curious U-shaped piece of wood that was used as a stool in the day and a pillow at night, to protect their mud packs.

But the Christians, Pete noticed, were wearing European-style clothes, as were most Kenyans. He found that disappointing, especially in that climate.

'Why do they change, Art?' he asked.

'There are several reasons, Pete, but the main one is that the men's beads and these heavy beautiful bead necklaces the women wear are not just decorations like the Masai ones. They are given for protection against evil spirits. Each danger these women face, they get another necklace. When a nurse weighed one lady's necklaces the other day that had been taken off her in hospital, she found that they weighed 15 kilos! So when someone comes to trust in Jesus to deliver them from evil, of course they take them off.'

Pete liked the Davises' simple house in Orus that Colin had helped build, with its two rooms, small shower and *choo*. The living room was divided in half by a bookcase, behind which they kept their paraffin fridge and stove, and where there was a sink and some cupboards for kitchen things. Entering the front door, on the left was the dining area with a window, outside which the Davises had put a bird table made from a hollowed meteorite. To the right were some locally made chairs and a radio.

Out beyond the bird table was Mary Ellen's netted vegetable garden and a little path that led to the three metal *rondavels* that Colin had also helped build from the kits that the Road Works Department supplied; that was where the three Davis children had their bedrooms.

That first afternoon, the girls cleaned up the house, Jeff and Pete went bird-watching and Colin went to check 'his' hill, the hill he was using for his research.

But the next few days were to be holiday. They all went camping for two nights. Pete had never been in such a place before, nor had he been hunting.

I went hunting with Jeff and the Pokot. I walked into a spider's web whilst stalking a guinea fowl and had a massive spider hanging off my cap. That night I slept on the Land Rover roof with Col and Jeff, which was a bit of a squash! Next day we walked to a river, which was high because of the rain. There were fresh buffalo tracks everywhere. We took spears. At the river we went 'tubing' in inner tubes (from the Land

Rover) which was fun. We spent nearly an hour on a mud bank, making slides and fighting.

Art went with them, enjoying all the fun! On the second evening he took them out in the Land Rover for game spotting with their spotlight. The next day they returned to Orus. The Davises and Colin had to get back to work, but Pete and Jeff, who was only a year older, spent some wonderful hours creeping through the bush trying to catch guinea fowl with pellet guns. Pete wrote, 'Jeff got one, but, me being a bad shot and having a faulty sight, I didn't get one. I got to within 3 yards of one, but I was out of pellets.'

On Saturday, the two of them walked over to 'Colin's hill'. This time they were bird-watching. Such birds there were, so different from others he had seen! The Go-Away bird, for example, and many others; squawking, calling, piping. The hill was called Kokwo Toto and Colin was to climb it every day for his research. It was south of Orus. Beside it, workers for Freedom from Hunger were putting in a dam for the cows. They had chosen this area because the previous year more underground water had been found here than at Orus. A male community health nurse had started a small dispensary and Colin was going to stay with him after Pete had left.

Pete got a lift home to Nairobi with a pastor the next day. We were thankful to see him. Again, he busied himself making his 'model' in his bedroom. Not until Christmas Day did we find out what he was doing. To our amazement we opened a most beautiful, detailed set of Persian and Assyrian chess soldiers that he had made with Fimo modelling clay. He had worked on it all that holiday, in a 'secret' workshop in his wardrobe that I never discovered!

15

Exploits!

Back at school it was no wonder that England seemed boring in comparison. The coming year was to be spent mostly working hard for his GCSEs in June. In between, however, Pete certainly played hard too.

One evening, in retaliation for some pranks Chris Foot had played on them, Pete and Karl managed to get into Chris's room one evening. Pete wrote:

We basically booby-trapped the place. If he opened a desk drawer, gravel would fall on his feet, if he opened his clothes drawers they were all upside down; if he opened a cupboard, water would fall on the floor. There was sugar in his bed, vaseline on his bed and chair, and toothpaste underneath his desk. We left a note on a charred piece of paper. It should be quite funny.

The friendly 'war' lasted most of the term.

Two of his friends had been upgraded to 'living out' (sleeping in another house). It meant they had fewer restrictions. Pete slept on the floor there one night for fun! Saturdays seem to have been the day to really let loose. Once they put Aeroflot stickers on a friendly member of staff's front door, and a stink bomb under his door mat. Another time, feeling very bored, they were fooling around pretending to be gangs and turning lights off and on, when Pete, entering the drying room, saw loads of clothes.

So I got some Levi 501 jeans, stuffed them with rugby shirts, stuck a hockey stick up for support and put a first eleven hockey shirt on the top. For a head, I used a swimming club cap and a long scarf. The HPs (Hyper Juvies) – we were in different groups ranging from the Black Berries to Rebel Contras and Hit Trio – thought it was 'wicked', so we put it on our shoulders.

The lights carefully turned out again, they hoisted their 'man' upstairs and left him in a bathroom, locking the door and climbing out of the window. There were queues of boys waiting outside the washroom that evening, including a rather pompous prefect. Finally, someone climbed in from outside. There was much laughter in the house that night! However, next morning, it transpired that the hockey stick and shirt belonged to one of the 'mega lads' who was 'not impressed'. Another boy, who had ambitions to become a prefect, persuaded the prefects to do a massive search for the culprits. Pete's two Indian friends were heavily interrogated but produced a convincing alibi. Pete added, 'Luckily, it died out, nobody was punished – had they been, that was the point at which we were going to own up.' (Woe to mothers who read Kipling's *Stalkey and Co.* to their offspring!)

Karl recalls other exploits of Pete's during that year:

While Pete's interest lingered away from his studies during class one day, he stumbled across an intriguing discovery. There was something hidden behind the moveable chalk board. Upon closer investigation after class, Pete met with an old fire exit leading up on to one of the turrets of the central tower of the main school building. The drama room was, in point of fact, the highest classroom in the school, located at the top of the central tower with turrets forming each corner.

The key for the door was in a fire safe in the vicinity. We couldn't quite go as far as breaking the glass, in case there was an alarm wired up. So how were we to get the key? Pete accidentally solved that mystery when he discovered that the little red box was a dud that could easily be unscrewed. We heard through the grapevine that one of the windows in a basement classroom was left open for those who dared to sneak out of the adjacent boarding house after hours. Alas, we were in.

The next obstacle was the motion detector for the hall lights. If the lights went on we would have some explaining to do. From experiments in between classes, we found that we could walk along the sides of the corridor without detection; however we first had to, very carefully, open the door without triggering the detector. Once past the infrared minefield we climbed five flights of stairs and on the third flight we encountered a hardworking professor in his office with the door open. We slipped past unnoticed. Sure enough the case unscrewed and the key dropped to the floor. It was quickly picked up and forced into a dark, rusted hole. The thick iron door swung open with a loud screech and we squeezed through the opening. Inside was a narrow corridor of stairs spiralling up to a second iron portal. We crawled up through the darkness and gently opened the door to the heavens. We were greeted with a spectacular view. We saw past the town far into the night in all directions.

The fresh, cool air carried the smell of recently cut grass and we felt like we were on top of the world, and indeed we were. While we were consumed with our personal high [just 'fantastic view', Pete wrote] we happened to look down as our professor friend was calling it a night. A whisper caught his attention and he turned to listen to the wind. To our surprise, it was the Deputy Headmaster! For a brief moment my heart stopped. I cringed with fear as if I had been caught for the stunt we had pulled that night. The feeling soon dispersed and I was overwhelmed by pride and arrogance after realising we had got away with the crime.

Pete wrote in his journal that they had also been in *'full combat gear, not very subtle!'*

Another day, in the same clothing, they crawled through the headmaster's garden in the dark. On yet another occasion they crept through barbed wire into the completely forbidden burnt-out school chapel. Pete had watched the fire with interest until *'all the priceless stained glass windows fell out'*, but added, *'it was quite sad'*.

On the last night of term he was caught on the fire escape by Mr Pendered, his housemaster. We did not hear what the consequences were but they cannot have been too severe; Mr Pendered later wrote of Pete that 'he spread so much innocent happiness around him'. On Pete's report that term, outstandingly well written as usual, after speaking of his academic hopes for Pete, his housemaster added, 'Peter . . . adds immensely to the happiness of the house.'

Karl and Pete had also discussed the future together. Karl wrote:

Pete, Rupert and I qualified for rugby's fifth team . . . by the month of November our practices were usually

cancelled, weather permitting. However on this particular
cold and crispy afternoon, our keen and eager coach had
somehow managed to secrete a splash of adrenaline from
his afternoon lunch and ordered us to report to Hemingway
14 – the farthest, most abandoned field on the corner of
the school property – for a freak practise. The field was
frozen solid and had been for a couple of weeks. Large
grooves and bumps had formed just right of the field due
to excessive weathering of the terrain, which gave Pete
and I the opportunity to flee the boring and monotonous
bonding session. The hardest part of our elusive plan was
to make sure we were on opposite teams. This way the
numbers on either team would remain the same once we
had disappeared . . . Before we were discovered, due to a
misguided pass which brought both teams to our camp,
Pete and I continued our childish debate on the better
of our two homelands. However, this time we decided
that the only way to settle the argument would be to visit
both countries.

They decided that during their year out after high
school, they would spend May and June in Kenya and
then fly to Montreal and have two months there. Later,
Rupert also was cajoled into joining them. They worked
out a great tour at a very good price. I think Pete might
have had misgivings because of the price, but it was
fun to discuss. And two years away was a lifetime.

The big family news that year was the arrival of
Rebecca, Jonathan and Sharon's first child and Pete's
first niece. He saw her twice in the January term and
was very amused by his brother filming every episode
of her tiny life. He had stayed in Rozi's flat, which had
been truly given her by God: Jonathan and Sharon had
put her up in their living room for over a month before
she found it. (It had been a strenuous time for her
anyway, as she was working full time and studying in

the evenings to become a chartered accountant.) Colin had visited them there too, and they had all had a great time putting up new wallpaper for her 'and filling my hair with glue', Pete wrote. And he had gone out and bought his first Swiss Army penknife.

From a Christian point of view, it was a year of consolidation but not much spark. In the autumn he wrote:

> Seriously, it's amazing how much praying one has to do; everyday someone comes up with a problem. I don't pray half enough. I get up in the morning at 7.00, have a shower and then read and pray for 15 minutes. The other day I fell asleep praying in the armchair in our study. The guy in my study is asking me how he could believe in a God. He's a Muslim but says that, apart from the basics e.g. be good and nice, he can't see much in it. But I really felt God gave me something to say to him.

At half-term Pete was very encouraged by staying with his godfather, my brother Richard, and Christian cousins, having great fun and also many good talks. Also, the time spent with his brothers and sister at weekends, and seeing a group of Christian students in Southampton who lived with Colin in a rented house (known as The Castle), helped him keep steadfast for the Lord, even though at that time his Christian life still seemed to be compartmentalised.

He wrote that the Christian Fellowship at school 'started thinking that it wasn't going all right, but nothing really happened'. He went to church with Rozi or Jonathan when he was with them, but spent most of his other Sundays hiking with Rupert and his other friends after compulsory chapel.

Perhaps not surprisingly, in view of all his other activities, he did badly in his 'mock' exams in November. But by the time the real exams came round in June he had worked hard to catch up and hoped he had done a little better.

I arrived in England at midnight on a Friday near the end of June, feeling rather under the weather: my plane had had to land in Cyprus with engine problems, and I'd had food poisoning. Jonathan, Sharon, Rozi and Colin and our precious new baby Rebecca all came to meet me. I was taken back to Jonathan's wonderfully renovated house for the rest of the night, then Jonathan, Sharon and Rebecca took me to 'Skinner's Day', the last day of the Tonbridge School year.

It felt odd being a grandmother and it was a surprise to see Pete in a suit. After admiring the beautiful little girl in her pink striped hat, I spent most of the day being shown the carefully-constructed toys that Pete had made in his woodwork exam and which had earned him an A grade. I was also introduced to his friends.

Pete said a sad goodbye to Karl, who was leaving to finish his schooling in Canada. Another goodbye, for Mr Pendered, followed – a strawberry tea at Judde House. It was the end of another era. He had been such a help to both Colin and Pete.

We visited my brother in Tunbridge Wells and then returned to London. I had come over for three reasons: to see Rebecca, for Pete's end of term, and to go, the following Saturday, to Colin's graduation. Sadly Julian could not be with me.

I hoped Pete would stay in London with me at Jonathan's to go to the graduation, but no way was he going to stay in England a day longer than necessary!

So on Sunday morning Rozi came to pick up Pete and me, to see him off at Heathrow. I thought he would be bored back at home, as Julian was very busy in the office. However, he wrote in his journal that he had a nice time lazing around, finishing some models and going out with Julian on any trips he had to make. On the Saturday he went by himself to a good rugby match, and visited a cousin.

Later he wrote what a watershed that time had been, all by himself with his father.

16

Inside Out! Experiencing the Living God

Since the children had passed the early 'putting to bed' stage, we had always tried to make sure we had a reading from the Bible and prayers together after supper every evening. When the troublesome teens started, we adopted the idea (I think from a book) that each evening one person in the family, however rebellious they might be at the time, was responsible for organising the prayers. They might not choose to do anything themselves, but it was their task to appoint someone to open in prayer, someone to read the Bible passage, someone to read out the questions in any book of study notes we might be following and someone to pray at the end. We found that even the most rebellious child did not mind doing this, and would usually even take part in the discussion.

When Pete had to write about his 'spiritual growth' for his Youth With A Mission entrance papers two years later, he wrote of his family and of this special time with Julian by himself:

> The foundation that God has given me to my Christian life, I'm sure, is my family. As I

have already mentioned, my parents, my two brothers and sister are committed Christians. They are all much older than me and I have a great respect for them. Seeing God work in their lives has been a continual assurance and encouragement to me.

In July 1989, I really began to realise the significance of Christianity in life. I was alone with my father, in Nairobi, for a week. During that time, in the evenings, we studied Romans together. It was then that I understood, really, why Christ came to earth, and how we can do nothing to redeem ourselves.

He added that, although he was sure that at Spring Harvest in 1986 he had come into a new experience of the infilling power of the Holy Spirit, it was during the beginning of this holiday that he spent a whole morning alone reading a simple book on the release of the Spirit and prayed the prayer at the end; and the Lord answered him and gave him an unmistakable 'baby gift', as Derek Prince would call it, that confirmed what the Lord had done. He wrote, 'That was tremendous encouragement and got me very excited.'

He did not say anything about it to us at the time. Perhaps his natural reticence was the reason, or the lack of the right opportunity. Of that time he notes in his journal, 'Mum is very busy with loads of refs' (refugees who came to our house). But back in England, later, he saw the book in Rozi's flat.

'That was the book I read at home,' he told her. 'It was through that book that I found out about asking for that gift.'

Colin and I soon arrived back in Kenya. Pete still fiercely wanted to have his family to himself. However, the next few weeks were spent going round with Colin, who was helping with the arrangements for some friends from his university who were hitchhiking round Kenya. Pete felt very frustrated with Colin because of this, especially when he also invited this couple to come to join us – though not actually in the house – in Mombasa for the family holiday later on. He tried to express his feelings to Colin, 'but got lost for words'. Colin was not pleased. But later, Pete wrote, 'I began to realise what hospitality is all about.'

Another family friend, Tim, also visited Kenya that July. In the last week of his visit he wanted to go to a game park. We encouraged him to go to Amboseli Game Park, which not only has a good quantity of game but also has the marvellous backdrop of Kilimanjaro, the largest mountain in Africa, with its dazzling snow cap that often appears to be floating in the sky above the clouds.

Colin and Pete went to a travel agent to try to make the arrangements for him and organise the hire of a car. An hour before Tim was due to leave, he said, 'Can't you two come too?' There was a great flurry to get Dad's permission and collect sandwiches, tent, food for the night and all the rest. I waved them cheerfully off to go on this extra, surprise adventure. They had a wonderful time. Tim's hired car managed the thirty miles of seriously dusty, lonely road that one hits after the tarmac ends in Namanga, and they arrived at the game park entrance well before dark. Tim had been booked into a nearby hotel. He left Colin and Pete at a campsite.

We put the tent up and made the fire after getting some wood. We decided not to sleep outside, after a discussion, on the grounds that mosquitoes would be a problem (a good excuse at least). We had a great supper of baked beans and scrambled egg cooked together, mandazi [type of Kenyan doughnut] and chai [tea leaves boiled together with milk and sugar in a saucepan. Delicious!]. So that was tasty. We could see zebra as it got dark, so used the extra tent poles as a snare which they could knock over so wake us up. It was a fantastic full moon as well. We went to bed.

There was a beetle just under the flysheet near the door which was only done up with some safety pins, which I was convinced was a snake. However I soon got to sleep. I woke about 3.30 and needed the loo. There was the continual chomp, chomp of the Zebra outside etc. We heard a lot of hyena, and elephant trumpeting. As I went out, all the zebra galloped away. I got in and slept for another two hours.

That night may not seem so remarkable, but to Colin and Pete, it was. The last time Colin had slept in a tent in a game park, again in a sheltered campsite with a ranger who lived there; he had woken at night and seen an elephant nearby. There were two other 18-year-old boys in the tent with him; they had silently watched the elephant. Elephants usually just graze and move on. This one, however, was curious about the tent, and after removing the flysheet, had, with his trunk, picked up the main tent, which had a sewn-in floor, with all of them in it. The elephant deposited it about fifteen metres away, treading on Colin's shoulder in the process – mercifully without applying its full weight, but breaking the collar bone and cracking the shoulder blade. Thankfully, they survived. But it made us all very wary of game-park camping.

Next day they woke to a beautiful morning, with the immense bulk of Kilimanjaro emerging from the clouds for an hour or so. They got their fire going to cook *chai* to accompany their Weetabix. Then Tim arrived and they embarked on a remarkably good drive round the park and saw a great quantity of game (Colin teasing Pete about his fear of buffalo). Then Tim took them to lunch at the hotel before the drive back north to Nairobi.

Pete was trying to see what life was like after the sheltered life of GCSEs. He was still only 16, while Colin was 22, so watching how Colin reacted to things was very important to him, and he was warmed by Tim's generosity. As Julian and I were very busy, the two of them had several opportunities to do things together.

One day they went by *matatu* (a form of private transport in Kenya, usually a minibus or covered pick-up, that are usually a law to themselves on the road and drive furiously) to Kijabe to visit the Davises' son, Jeff. On the way home, squashed for an hour in the back of a car, Pete felt free to talk to Colin about life in Tonbridge. He mentioned the idea that Karl, Rupert and he had had about their year off: the Kenya/Canada trip. The next day, the three of them borrowed our car for an outing to Naivasha. There was thick cloud on the escarpment road as they wound down into the Rift Valley. Pete wrote later, '"Someone" kept the car in good order. We saw three cars which had gone into the back of each other on the top which looked pretty nasty.' His description of that trip is full of wry humour, especially over his brother's interest in birds, but also pointing out his own mistakes:

We saw one of the phantom birds of prey just outside a Masai boma which looks like a cross between a so and so but isn't. So we looked at that a lot. Before we struck the main road, we found a giraffe mama with two babies who were 'cute' – Jeff's terminology – and one had only recently been born, still with its umbilical cord on it. After that we drove on to the main road and stopped to search for lammergeier. We saw one bird of prey which Colin said immediately, 'That's a Verreaux's eagle. You can tell them so certainly when you see one, they are very obvious,' so Jeff was pleased as he had not seen one before. Then it landed and Jeff asked, 'Um. Col. Why does it have a red tail? . . .' it turned out to be an Augur buzzard. I think Jeff and I made some amusing comments (we thought so) on that afterwards. We drove on and I was determined to get them to the gorge. So we finally got to the usual place after following many of my, 'I'm sure this is the road, um . . . Yes I'm sure it is, well maybe not, um . . .'

Another time, they went with Julian and some visitors to the place where Peter Cameron Scott was buried. He had had a vision for a mission that would preach the good news of Jesus Christ across Africa, from Mombasa right across to Chad. He arrived at the Kenyan coast in 1895 and died eighteen months later from malaria. He was only 29 years old, but he had lived long enough to pass on the vision to others to get the Africa Inland Mission started.

Julian had a committee meeting there, so the two boys drove around the area for a while. Pete noted 'the beautiful little old church there built out of sun-baked bricks.'

They called in at a Bible college nearby on their way home. Pete was very impressed with what the principal had achieved in building with so little funds, and also with the fact that after they had been shown around, all the students came up to where they were, singing *'Tembea na Yesu'* ('Walk with Jesus'), and then told them where each of them had come from.

That was Monday. 'On Tuesday morning,' he writes, 'I took the book *Release of the Spirit* and read it in the morning. I understood it all and it was just so good. I was really chuffed in God after that. It was the 24.7.89. I know that because it's written down in my *Biblia* [Bible] beside me here. It was great.'

During the next week Colin's friends, mostly from Southampton University, arrived in Nairobi. Colin and Pete went out with them and took them to get buses etc. Pete was conscious that they were all older than he was, though they were very kind to him. But he had found a great treasure, in that Jesus was able and willing to help in his insignificant problems. On one occasion they were playing a game: they each had to supply the next sentence, by turn, in a developing story. 'It was really good,' Pete recalled, 'because previously, in games like that, I'd usually say something really dumb, which was not funny. But if I prayed before my turn, God gave me something which wasn't stupid, at least.'

Rozi arrived from England. 'It was such fun her coming home,' Pete recorded. And then we packed for our yearly trip to the coast.

It was a memorable one that year. We had about twelve of Rozi's or Colin's friends staying or camping near us. As we had some unseasonal rain, we had fifteen or so for most meals!

The first four days, however, we were by ourselves. Colin and Pete messed about with the papyrus boat that we had previously brought from Lake Baringo, and Rozi floated on a lilo. Then suddenly everything changed, and Pete's brother and sister just wanted to entertain their guests. Pete felt rather left out, like William in Richmal Crompton's famous children's books, and was often left walking on the beach by himself. He began to learn how to cope feeling somewhat out of things. But he didn't need to for long! When other friends appeared, especially Polly who later married his cousin, he was welcomed by them all.

But at least four times in his journal he mentions praying when at a loss as to what to do, and the Lord showed him:

My frustration had died down quite a bit and I had really prayed about it. And I just talked to one of them and it was just so hajabu [amazing, miraculous]! One thing which is incredible and gets my emotions going is a bright moon on a white beach + palm trees. I felt wonderful and got on really well just chatting.

That leg of the holiday over, he wrote: 'It was really sad saying bye-bye. It was really good they had come along and I had learnt a lot about hospitality from all the maneno [discussion, debate, consultation, argument]. I got on very well with them in the end.'

Back in Nairobi, with some of the Mombasa group and others like Kate Peppiatt and her brother David (generally known by his Swahili name, Daudi) who had joined them, he and the others pooled their resources and planned a safari on their own, going to Amboseli Game Park again, and then west to Eldoret and north to Pokot country to show it all to their friends.

Pete began to learn three big lessons in that time.

First, he learned that God was taking care of them. Comparatively little things such as Julian encouraging him to drive as we went together to Mombasa boosted his confidence. Then, on the first leg of their safari there were two big instances of God caring for them.

The party of eight needed two 4 x 4 vehicles. It was so late into the high season for tourists that it was very hard to hire good ones cheaply, but they got the best they could. Pete wrote of them:

> One of the back wheels was about an inch lower than the other; the doors didn't close properly; the windscreen wipers didn't work; the headlights just rattled around; the radiator supports were broken and very weak; the windows didn't open properly; the tread on the tyres was about bald – and a lot more, like the battery was strapped on and the fuel gauge was broken. But we packed up, prayed and set off.

They limped out of our drive after lunch to go to Amboseli. I waved them off and prayed!

They stopped for a picnic tea before they left the tarmac. As they were returning to the vehicles they realised, to their horror, that one of the only car keys had fallen into the long grass. After a huge search there was still no sign of it.

> Daudi quickly said that we could hot-wire it, an experienced car thief!! Well we looked and some people got very worried. Then we all stopped, got

together, and prayed. Daudi went to where one of the others had just been looking and found it immediately. I think it was God's little way of saying, certainly to me, that if we wanted a good time we were going to have to trust him only. It was jus' swell.

They hurried on, leaving the tarmac at Namanga and joining the dirt road for the rest of the way.

We started down the fatal road. It was awful, especially in those cars – absolutely woeful. Well for the first 20 mins, I just prayed, very earnestly, but then just stopped and talked to Kate. She asked me how far it was to go, and thought it very funny when I said, 'Round the corner and then another three hours.' Well, as we bombed along we saw this stopped thing way ahead; 'Doreen' [two of the young men in the party had been nicknamed Doreen and Fanny] had overtaken us previously, it was Doreen and car. So we stopped, and the battery had fallen out so Colin was strapping it back in with a cut-up coat hanger. The radiators were also being held up solely by the coat hangers. Everybody took time to disappear in the hedge and when we got bored, me and Woly (or Polly and I) went snake hunting. I hadn't been as solemn as perhaps I could have been.

And then we drove across the lake [a sand lake which fills with water only in heavy rain] and Kili [the mountain, Kilimanjaro] appeared. I was happy, wonderfully and really heartened. Doreen's load slowed down, and I waved at them and told them their car was going sss . . . sss . . . sss and must have a puncture, but they all thought that I was just being silly, so just drove on, which was really nasty; and I was never really silly. Well, soon they realised it and stopped. I jumped out and said, 'What an incredible place to have a puncture!' It was, absolutely hajabu. But Doreen wasn't so satisfied and I think someone may have looked at me in that 'Wot-a-tiresome-little-boy' way, e.g. Wozi. But when we found that the spare had a puncture as well, I really thought it was hilarious but was a good boy and subdued my feelings a little as I thought it was necessary.

We used the spare from the other car and drove straight to the park lodge. We gave the wheel to the fundi. Col and Daudi [the Swahili version of David] sat at the back of the lodge for a while, with the cars, while we went to the front and the girls washed their faces and Doreen and I discussed the hunting season on the porch with our lime and Malibu.

'They all,' said Pete, 'splayed out on the porch and were so tired they did not even see the sign saying "Residents only".' They enjoyed the beauty of Kilimanjaro in front of them and 'the sight of an African cat stalking its prey to the sound of the workers playing football, and the ref's whistle.' There was an amazing sunset, which they all went out to look at. Pete said, 'My mind boggled . . . the colours were extraordinary; they were incredible. Someone should have tried to tell me there was no God then!'

Because of the puncture they arrived in the official campsite after dark. There were other campers there, so they parked on the opposite side. Unfortunately, in the rush to leave our house they had forgotten to take the hurricane lamps, so the first thing to do was to collect firewood and get a big blaze going. They ate some great stew that the girls cooked in the dark over the fire and put up the tents in a horseshoe formation. Pete and Daudi's borrowed tent was next to the fire, then Colin's (a toy tent from home!), then the three ladies' and then Doreen and Fanny's. They sat round the fire for some time singing, with Colin accompanying on the guitar, then made preparations for bed. According to Kate, 'The boys were trying to wind us up, by telling us all the awful stories they could think of.' Pete added, 'Hyena howled round us and we saw a lot of eyes, all probably African wild cats. Daudi got really excited. There was some hooting and shouting from somewhere in the camp which was a bit worrying, but then it was a long way off, and we had a fire.'

Kate: 'We then started to get ready for bed and we three girls went into the "bushes". The boys started calling us to come back. We thought they were teasing us again at first but then recognised the urgency in their voices and moved back fast.'

Pete: 'Daudi and I shone a torch round and saw an elephant, just a grey-black hulk about a hundred metres away. People started shining torches at it and I got a bit fed up as I wanted to go to bed and honestly thought that if we shut up, it would come to look for food and be really fun, it walking near our tents [one had done this when some friends of ours were there].'

So Pete climbed thankfully into his tent and wriggled into his sleeping-bag, back towards the tent wall. Daudi was trying to settle on the other side. The others were also quietening down, but Pete was just conscious of his sister opening the car door as she needed its mirror and meagre light to fix her 'eyeballs' (contact lenses).

Daudi, a little on edge, whispered to a sleepy Pete, 'It's getting very close now, you can hear its breathing.'

'Yeah, yeah.' Pete didn't take much notice.

'Pete! Can't you see it!'

Pete could. 'I looked out and saw a grey shape about twenty yards away on the other side of the track. So I said, "It is closer." 'He had been looking out of a small gap in the tent flap. As he spoke he looked round to the left – and to his shock realised that what he had first seen had been a bush, and that the elephant – 'that black shape which is bigger at the top than the bottom' – was just three metres away!

'Daudi! Daudi!' he whispered in a kind of screaming whisper. 'It's only three metres away.'

It all seemed to be happening in slow motion after that. Daudi thought the elephant sounded angry. They could hear its heavy breathing getting louder, and the hurried flump, flump of its feet. Pete felt he should tell the girls, who were still whispering and zipping up their tent flaps, to be quiet, but *my body had seized up, expecting a crushing pressure – my head was nearest, that wasn't so nice*.

Suddenly, the boys felt their whole tent lurch, and Pete felt the elephant's leg pressing on his back. Then its trunk hit the aluminium crossbar of the tent. There was a great crash and the tent crumpled down onto the boys.

Rozi, in the car, saw what was happening. She put her hand on the horn – which just went 'peep!' Colin also heard, and rushed out immediately, shouting, 'Get out of your tents!' Kate scrambled out after Polly into the bright moonlight. 'It looked,' she wrote, 'as if the elephant had trampled the boys. Colin looked so small, with a bit of stick in his hand, as he walked towards the elephant.'

'Boy, have I got a brother!' Pete wrote later. 'I had got into a kneeling position and just yelled Jesus!'

But when he heard Colin shout, 'Get out of your tents', he unzipped the flap – 'and saw those big kicking grey feet, with flickering firelight on them. Daudi saw its tusks as it backed up with its tusks low. I didn't hang around to observe the spectacle, but my big brother just stood there and yelled, "IN THE NAME OF JESUS, GO AWAY. WHAT DO YOU THINK YOU ARE DOING? GO AWAY."'

To their astonishment, the huge creature backed into the bush. Pete was shaking like a leaf; they had been within inches of being trampled. He added wryly, 'Doreen and Fanny had been in their little peapod and by the time they'd undone the zips and de-sealed the pores to normal atmospheric pressure, then got out, the elephant had vanished.'

They spent the rest of the night nearer the 'noisy tourists'!

According to the warden, the elephant had been 'a rogue bull' and 'seemed nervous'. We heard that, tragically, some other tourists were killed there the following week.

On the second leg of their safari to western Kenya, they did manage to get slightly better vehicles, but they had other 'incidents'.

One day, when all their gear was still soaking wet from the previous night's camping and they were very behind schedule, having made a brief call at

Pete's instigation into Turi, and when they saw the unseasonably heavy clouds gathering again, God gave them an idea: if it is raining on Mount Elgon, it will be miserable and we are well late, so let's go to Auntie Patty's.

Patty Drakely, Rozi's godmother, was one of those remarkable people one encounters only rarely. After gaining an OBE for founding an excellent teachers' college in Uganda, she came to help at Mosoriot Teachers' College while we were there. Then the Lord had called her, much to her mission's loving consternation (she was well past retirement age) to invest all her savings in a small house with beautiful grounds in the highlands at Kaptagat, about ten miles out of Eldoret, to make a place available for tired Christians to rest, in particular those escaping the heat of Uganda. Rozi said that she was sure Auntie Patty would let them camp there, though Pete confessed that, 'I'm sure that she was hoping, certainly I was, that there might be room in one of the boarding houses.'

Patty kept her home beautifully and used her family bone china and silver. She was always up to date with world news and had the gift of making beautiful gardens. Her rooms were filled with lovely chintzes and pictures – some of which were her own oil paintings – and huge bowls of flowers; but most of all she really loved the Lord.

It was dark. Rozi and Colin apprehensively went first. They knocked on the door, and were lovingly welcomed by Patty. 'I was so pleased to see them again,' she told me later.

Then Rozi said, 'There are a few more of us outside.'

'Tell them to come in at once, I will get some tea made for you,' Patty cheerfully replied. She was very amused when eight of them filed in! She lovingly opened up a guesthouse for the night for them.

Two years later, Pete wrote to YWAM:

'I was particularly struck while visiting an 89-year-old lady. She was a tremendous saint. I was totally awed when she said with such sincerity that in 80 years of being a Christian, God had never let her down. Of course it says that in the Bible, and that alone is an amazing promise. Yet the way she said it, so simply, meant a lot to me.'

I hope that dear Patty is reading this in heaven!

Pete saw many other instances of God's great care on that safari: on their trip up to Orus – Pokot again – especially when they had to give a lift to armed hunters in the dark; or the time when Pete, Rozi and Kate were alone and ran into major difficulties with the vehicle, and God sent them help.

Secondly, Pete began to learn how to cope with loneliness. It came over him when it seemed that those in the other tent were having all the fun.

The Toyota lot laughed and laughed and I went to sleep a little sad. I woke up quite a lot in the night, but I slept all right. I woke up eventually while it was still dark, got up and went to the choo. The Toyota people were already laughing again. After that I went beyond the bank, where I was away from things and waited as it got light and listened to the birds singing below. It was really beautiful, but I wasn't so very happy and prayed about everything and thought about it. I decided, and I'm sure I was right, that I was certainly the youngest there in feeling and atmosphere. I don't know . . . it was difficult to know what to do.

They travelled hundreds of miles in the very unreliable vehicles that they had rented. Pete, being the smallest, often had to squash into the back. 'The people in the front had a very merry time which was good . . . But I felt little again. Eventually I got very juvenile in order to stop getting depressed . . . We got singing.'

I believe that the Lord answered his prayer by changing Pete's mind so that he didn't wallow in self-pity. Things went better after that.

Thirdly, he learnt the importance of spending time with God each day. He was with Christians who, to get their quiet times with God, sat on the roof of the vehicles, disappeared into the bush for a time, or went on *Jambo Mungu* (*Jambo* is a Swahili greeting that means 'What's the affair?' It is the Kenyan 'Hello'. *Mungu* means 'God') walks – Daudi's speciality. The fellowship with them was very encouraging.

Each evening, too, they sang and prayed together round the camp fire. It all demonstrated that it is possible to be a young person and also be radical in your Christian life.

Yet Pete had a secret question in his heart that would not appear until his time with YWAM.

17

The Lower Sixth Form:
'God is So Incredible'

When he finally arrived back in Nairobi Pete found his GCSE results waiting for him. To his delight, he had achieved five grade As, three Bs and a C. The next week, he was back at Tonbridge with the status of a sixth-former. To our surprise, he had not been made a prefect.

'Funny sort of housemaster, not to make you a prefect, Pete,' I said to him.

'No Mum – not at all,' he replied. 'I'm sure he did it to help me. Actually I have much more influence in the house not being a prefect.'

By his own admission he didn't work so hard that term and, except for geography had poor end-of-term results. That, he felt, was largely because he spent so many hours writing up all they had done that wonderful summer in his journal. Not very wise, I suppose, but I'm very thankful for it now!

He was determined to spend more time in prayer and reading his Bible. He missed Karl, and Rupert had developed other interests. He felt motivated to pray regularly for six of his friends, and became more interested in the youth group at the local church. Its leader told me, 'If I saw a bunch of folk at our gatherings, I could be sure Pete was in the middle of them.' He had a profound effect on several of the young people there. He had the gift of being able to mix easily with people no matter where they came from, and he did not put on airs because he was at a boarding school.

He wrote to one of the young people, whom he knew had been feeling discouraged:

> I don't want to preach or anything, but because I know God is so great and his love so, so infinite and that he longs for us not to be depressed. I was really, really challenged by Philippians 4:4, 'Rejoice in the Lord always.' What a verse! But God means it I'm sure.
>
> I had a period of depression when I wasn't getting on with anyone. I realised that I had no real friends apart from one who was in South America and that really made me depressed. And one evening I was thinking about it all, then just got praying about it, and it's difficult to explain but I felt in my mind this voice, or thought, which said, 'But I am your friend.'
>
> It blew my mind. Whoever more could we wish for but Jesus?

'As I look back on that letter,' recalls its recipient, 'Pete seems on the one hand as any other teenager of the time, young and daft, but he had this other "level", a deeper understanding of the character of Jesus.'

As a cadet in the school's Navy Corps,[6] he had fun windsurfing and spent two weekends away. One was at an army camp, where he fired some large guns; his shoulder ached after that. 'Not what I joined the Navy for,' he wrote – which is interesting, given his

huge interest in war machines and guns as a small
boy. The second weekend was at camp in the Brecon
Beacon hills, and involved day hikes on army rations.
He loved it. One big thrill was finding that the boy
he was walking with was a strong Christian. He also
had some good exeats with his brother and sister in
London, but half-term was very special, because his
godfather (my brother, Richard Salmon) took him with
his family and another cousin's family to their cottage
at Land's End, and then on to his parish weekend.
Cornwall put school out of his mind for a while – '*I
had fun there sitting on Aire Point watching the
amazing waves smash in*' – but the parish weekend
was the highlight for Pete.

'*I learnt so much about MY God. Wow! Nick
Faraday was really good, and, so was Greg
and me finishing off all the trifles etc. God is
so incredible; here I learnt a lot, and how little I
knew him.*

'*I got back to school at 12 a.m. So Sandy* [the
housemaster] *wasn't so happy.*'

He spent his 17th birthday with Rozi in her flat. We
had told him he would get his present from us in the
holidays.

In one of his letters he hinted that he would like a
camera for Christmas. He had been doing some good
art, and he had managed some good photos with the
cheap camera we had given him earlier, but he needed
a better one, especially for his geography project.

When he came out to Kenya we were all very excited,
for Jonathan and Sharon were bringing out their
beautiful baby Rebecca to join us for the holiday. Pete
was amazed at how much she kept her parents awake!

On Christmas Day, relatives joined us. In the
afternoon, back at home, Pete was again Father

Christmas. It was our family custom, most Christmases, to have someone dressing up in Dad's dressinggown and our ancient mask, much to the amusement of our many guests. Everybody received a present. Pete said, 'I really enjoyed that.' The visitors left and everyone except him went for a walk. He was busy wrapping up his last family presents – to be opened again round the fire that evening!

We began to unwrap them about 6.00 p.m. [Pete wrote in his journal]. My first one was a rucksack. My heart sank, as I had so wanted a camera. It was my birthday present really, but this had cost £36 and so would Mum and Dad pay more than that for a camera as well? So I was really sad while trying to look happy. I had prayed for one, a bit guiltily, as I thought that was a bit naughty (because of the price).

Then I said to myself, 'Well I'm told to rejoice in everything'. So, as I did that, I was handed a box which had a Pentax P30N body in it. Later I got a 28–80 mm lens. I couldn't believe it! What a sense of humour God has; and what great parents and bros and sis I've been given. I can't understand why, but God's done it and I would love to serve him so much more in my life. I don't understand why my God is so good. Anyway, the camera was much more expensive than expected from Ma and Pa, so it's really for my 18th as well!

Actually, it was largely because of the tremendous generosity of his brother and sister. Photography was more than just fun for Pete. He had become very interested in the refugees who I was helping to care for, and had decided to make them the subject of his geography project, hence the need for a good camera. He took some excellent photos that holiday, in a shack that friends of mine lived in.

After Christmas we took all the family up-country, staying again with Patty. We stayed in her garden with Sharon and Rebecca while Jonathan took Pete for a trip up Mount Elgon, though they did not get as high as they had hoped, owing to the mud on the edges of the road. One corner just proved too hard for them, in spite of Jonathan's skilful driving and all the logs and other materials they put in the water. They walked on, past the tree line, but when Pete saw fresh buffalo droppings he encouraged his brother to go back fast! Later Jonathan hired a four-wheel drive Suzuki and took Pete onto the escarpment high above Lake Magadi and let him do quite a bit of the driving, which pleased him immensely. Rozi's Christmas holiday was so short that she stayed in England with friends. Colin was in Portugal with the A Rocha fellowship, where he was working as assistant warden. It was to be another year before we could all be together again.

18

The Navy and Courses: 'I Get Fed Up with Being Ripped Off'

Back at school, Pete was kept busy. Chemistry, especially, was giving him trouble, but he was having some fun too. He wrote to us:

I've had an amazing two weeks now. I had my first exeat with Uncle John and Gina. I don't know if I told you but they appointed me Rachel's godfather. I really enjoyed that weekend.

Then I did some wild windsurfing on the Tuesday in force 6 winds which was incredible. I loved it. The weekend was a bit laid back, then on Monday (a week ago yesterday), the school took the whole of the lower sixth, 120 of us, to Coventry. We visited the cathedral the first day, then I stayed in a guesthouse/bed and breakfast which was a wonderfully run down one, with 15 other people, in a room with a colour TV. Second day we visited a comprehensive school which was great; the pupils (or whatever) there took us to a pub for lunch. They were really fun people. Then we went ten-pin bowling in the afternoon.

That night, the boys in my room had a long discussion about drugs (one of them had tried some), then on families and then on life and death, etc. It was incredible, and terrible really to see what non-Christians thought. I gave my views. I've a lot to learn still.

On Thursday we went to an industry and then to a community centre where we saw some of the suffering that the unemployed go through in England.

Later, musing about that time in Coventry and of some of the suffering he saw in the community centre, he wrote in his journal:

I learnt there that:
- the best workers are self-motivated people
- the English are friendly
- both rich and poor suffer until they are Christians (I mean I knew that before but not so well)

That spring term, he started sailing with the Navy Corps, which he really enjoyed. Later a friend wrote:

As you remembered correctly, I sailed with Pete quite a bit in little 420s which are quite fast and notoriously unstable racing dinghies.

Typically we took a more laid back approach to the sailing than many of the others in the 20-strong club, often pottering around the reservoir enjoying a chat, gazing over towards the greens and ridge, under a watery, wintry sun, oblivious of all the earnest racing activity around us. When we did race we usually created a laugh or two, typically causing fair chaos amongst the rest of the competitors. I spent quite possibly the coldest 20 minutes of my life, with Pete, in the frigid waters of Bough Beech reservoir after capsizing on an extremely windy Saturday afternoon. The boat had gone turtle (that is, upside down) so getting it back up again was a fair challenge, involving lots of heaving on the centreboard, while balanced on a slippery hull. When it did come upright again with water pouring off the flogging sail, we were thrilled – only to see it get blown over before we could get in. After two more of these episodes we called it a day and got the rescue boat to give us a hand. Still they were great times we had on the water.

Other memories of Pete include going up to Leeds to see the university with him on an exceedingly cold December day. We met my grandfather's nephew – who teaches there – for lunch at his house. He's an extremely laid back academic and I think this, and the tour of the geography dept. made Pete keen on studying there.

His sailing friend also wrote, 'And, finally, what made Pete different? His passion for jazz, and all things Kenyan, his complete lack of pretension, his jokey, pranky manner, his anger at the building of more motorways in Britain and the human-scale he brought to life and his beliefs.'

Pete had given up working for music exams, but he still enjoyed his lessons and practise in the music school that the school had. It was a break from the usual routine. Even the master was from outside the school. During the holidays, he would tinkle away on the piano for a whole morning at a time. After taking Grade 5, he started concentrating on jazz, for which he had a special love: he may have felt it was connected with Africa. The headmaster wrote on one of his reports, 'I envy him his jazz piano technique.'

Half-term was hard. The son of the people he was staying with, who was a close friend of Pete's, had become involved with a godless crowd. Pete stayed up late one night praying for him. As he glanced up at the mantelpiece he saw the verse, *'If you believe, you will receive whatever you ask for in prayer'* (Matthew 21:22). He commented, 'Which I think is an amazing word of God. So I do believe he will really come back to God.'

He did feel lonely at school at times. He read his Bible for the last hour each night, and he prayed for his friends: especially the 'Big Six' – two from Turi, Karl, Rupert and two others from Tonbridge.

He did not write about it much but it is obvious that he was witnessing that he was a Christian. He writes of a boy he spoke to from another house at school whilst on another wet Welsh camp 'which was really cool'.

And sometimes Pete was discouraged.

It's 12.27 a.m. I should really be reading my Bible, but on the last four evenings I haven't been very motivated, so I'm just going to write my thoughts. I keep realising how hopeless life would be without God, but I don't find I am awestruck by it, just wondrous. Chemistry is really hard . . . the teacher unsympathetic. I wish my friends would become Christians. I'm really good friends with one at present and I'd love to talk to him about God but I'm worried that I will say the wrong thing at the wrong time, and as he's so negative to all I say, I'm waiting till I'm prompted to say something, but maybe I shouldn't. I get fed up with being ripped off by people in biology.

The head of house gave a talk tonight to the house, introduced 'Atheism'. It should really have been, 'How This School's Put Me Off

Christianity.' He basically, gave all his reasons why he didn't believe in God, put very bluntly, and with no subtlety. Querish got quite upset. He said things like 'How can Jesus say, "These will go to heaven, while Muslims won't"?' and all the other normal reasons. It's so terrible that people have such a warped idea of Christianity and God. I feel a fool for not witnessing more but I just feel now that that is all I want to do when I grow up. But of course God's got to guide me. I just thought I would put that down. I've only told Uncle John and Gina and Ruth Morris [a cousin who had just returned from a Youth With A Mission discipleship course, full of joy in God]. It's funny, my mind says I would love to do that but my heart feels indifferent to it, which I don't like. But if God really wants me to do that, he'll kindle a caring if I ask. Praise God. What a real God He is! . . . I took my first Bible Study in CF the other day on the parable of the sower. It was awful. I had prayed about it a bit but obviously not enough. My Bible readings have been pretty empty recently.

But there is a joyful note on this page, written six months later. 'Well. Hallelujah! The above has been conquered with Christ's victory now.'

But that was still in the future. Meanwhile, he was not looking forward to his biology field trip that came slap in the middle of the holidays; but he noted in his journal, 'Some of the boys were a bit cool, but God amazingly answered prayer. [Two of the boys] had been a bit nasty in biology, so I asked God that they wouldn't be like that in Cornwall and [one of them] was really nice. Praise God!'

Because the course came in the middle of the holiday, for the first time he did not have an opportunity to come to Kenya. He spent the first weekend with John and Gina for the christening of Rachel, his goddaughter. He wrote 'It's such an important and responsible thing, I've realised.' He prayed for her daily. Jonathan and Sharon then took him home for that week to work on their home improvements – for which they paid him very generously. (Pete commented, 'I'm not arguing with such a superior businessman!')

Colin had invited him to visit, and now he had a week more holiday and money in his pocket. 'Thursday morning I bought a 70-litre Karrier back pack [swapped for the inferior one we had given him for Christmas!], packed it, then Shaz [Sharon] dropped me off at Gatwick in the afternoon on her way to her mum's and I was now on my way to PORTUGAL.'

19

Portugal and God's Encouragement

Pete arrived at Faro Airport around 10.30 p.m. on a shabby plane, about an hour late. He collected his luggage and struggled through customs, to find his brother watching out for him through his binoculars. An hour's drive brought them to Mexilhoeira Grande where Colin was renting a room. 'The whole air stank of orange blossom as I climbed out, and it was warm and humid. I was immediately reminded of Mombasa. It was so good being with Col in this strange place which was his "house".'

It was small. Pete slept in a sleeping-bag on cushions on the floor and woke at 7.30 a.m. for breakfast with the landlady. 'The first thing I saw was a brilliant white wall with clean red tiles from the room opposite, with a clear blue sky behind it. Fantastic!'

He enjoyed his breakfast of Portuguese cornflakes, hot chocolate and French bread, and was really pleased to be in a proper Portuguese house. Afterwards they drove to the main A Rocha centre, about five minutes' drive away.

The wardens, Peter and Miranda Harris, had been very kind to Colin, who had adopted the Kenyan custom of calling Miranda the mother of her son, hence 'Mama Jem'. Pete wrote, 'I wandered through to the sitting-room, and Mama Jem came down the stairs and said, "You're not a fat little brother!" (which Col had vividly described me as the day before). It was really good meeting her.'

The next two days were spent with Col, taking some Liverpudlian geography students up into the mountains, holding a service at the centre on Sunday, and in the evening playing games with some of the folk who were staying.

We played 'Twister' in the sitting-room. It was so funny. But I was in a really low mood, because I had a real complex that I couldn't make conversation and was really bad at it and unfunny, etc., etc. But it was fun all the same. We were still there when the students (who had gone out to get 'stoned') got back, at 12, then me and Colin departed to our mansion.

He found that fitting identification rings to birds in the middle of the night, or day, was not really his cup of tea – he felt sorry for the birds! Daytime was not so bad; at least they could sunbathe. Fortunately, some of Colin's friends from university were visiting, and Pete was able to go off with them sometimes.

One afternoon he had another brush with death. Colin, his friends and some of the Harris children went to a water sports place.

It was just an enormous agglomeration of slides. I got very excited and ran up with Jem and Col. There was a scruntie girlie of a lifeguard at the top of the MOST DANGEROUS one, so that came up most frequently as the one to slide down . . . The highlight of the afternoon came when one of the friends, 'Q', and I were going down one together and he thought it would be amusing if he jumped on directly behind me. He did. So when I shot out at the bottom, I tried to get out of his way by stopping and jumping sideways. It didn't work. His chin came, flunk, pfwam, onto my head. To begin with we were sort of shocked. Then we sat there and cracked up. It seemed very funny. Col noticed blood in the pool about us. I saw a cut on Q, so immediately said it was his blood. He said he did not think it hurt too much. So we got out of the pool sniggering away when someone said, 'Are you sure you are not bleeding Pete?' They had seen a big red blob in my hair (it wasn't my hair) (PS God is good). I was bleeding; I had quite a big cut. So we went back to our towels, not sure what to do. I was sure I was fine, but a groundsman came up and directed us to a Red Cross place that we hadn't noticed. So we went in and found a dressed-up, large Portuguese woman who couldn't speak English. She looked at our heads then directed me to lie down on a bed. She then cut off some hair and sprayed something on the cut and whacked three stitches into it. I couldn't believe it. Q got it as well. I was amused. Mama Jem was not!

That was Good Friday; they had a special Portuguese Easter evening that day, with 'bready cakes' with whole boiled eggs in them. Then they 'read the Bible and sang. It was a very holy and lovely time I remember.'

Sunday morning was Easter. We all got up very early to get down to the end of the headland to have communion there. It was fantastic. The sun coming up; and singing was so majestic. It was a very good morning . . . I walked back along the marshes by myself, and loved it. It was a good time again. We got back to breakfast. I then had the fun of giving the Harrises an Easter egg I had brought for them, without being too daft. I probably was. Anyway, we had lunch then decided to go fishing . . . we caught ulra lettica – water cabbage – only. It did feel all a bit last-dayish and that evening at supper we had a service prayer time which was fantastic. Col and I and one other sang a Swahili song to the non-knowers – it was a bit prideful instead of praiseful. Sorry God. After a breakfast at A Rocha the next morning, I said farewell to the world, and got whacked into one of the old Portuguese trains at Cruzinia.

. . . That week has very fine memories . . . Probably it was highlighted by having had such a depressing field trip week. To put it basically, 'I was refreshed in God'. On the train back, I opened a small envelope which Col had thrust at me as I left. It was from the Harrises, with a £10 note in it and a swell letter.

Thank God for those who refresh the saints, even the little ones. Pete added:

I've missed out lots of special bits that I can't remember happened when. For instance, licking out the Harrises' cake tins, and looking round the flat; water-fighting with Jem; Mike getting told off by Mama Jem; Beth and Jem playing with bubbles on the back lawn with Beth popping them with a rainbow umbrella; talking to Mama Jem and Pete and some of the guests; having coffee in a small cafe right up Monchique; and walking with Beth [she was 6] along the road down to the sea, picking flowers. I mean, it was just a very good week.

But the most memorable thing, looking back later, was the morning before the accident. He had been very discouraged and had sat the day before, by the project's new fish pond ('frog bog puddle' Pete called it) 'and asked God a lot about it'. That morning, for once in history, the landlady's breakfast came late and Colin talked with him. 'Col told me about Hudson Taylor's book, where he just handed everything to God, as he could do nothing. It was just God shouting at me, and it worked, well.' Writing about it later he said:

I spent Easter with a brother at a Christian Field Study centre in Portugal. I had become quite depressed and cold in my prayer. One evening there, I really prayed about the mending of that weakness. The very next morning, my brother quite spontaneously began to tell me that he had suffered just like that. He then related how, through a book on Hudson Taylor, he had learnt just to commit those problems to God. Amazing! I did just that. The next term was the first term when I could claim I definitely grew in God whilst at school.

On return to England, in spite of feeling the cold, he was very conscious of answered prayer as he went on 'work experience' in London. It made him seriously think of doing geography, for his degree.

20

Summer Term 1990:
'I Began to Grow in God'

The summer term was to be a busy one.

> I got back to school and had all of my biology project to write up. I worked and worked. In fact I would even say I worked well. I had a small study on the ground floor of Judde, the same as I had all through the Lower 6th, and I sat in there for many hours. Every evening at 11, or later in the term 11.30, I would stop working, put on a Mungu [God] tape and have an hour's Bible study/read a good book and pray.

Towards the end of May he wrote to us:

> Hello, hello.
> Well I've finished! 130+ sides of this stuff (A4 paper) I'm writing on is graphed, diagrammed, resulted and written on. I finished my 'Life on the Rocky Shore' biology project this afternoon with only a photo to stick on a sheet of paper, of my biology teacher wandering across a huge sandy beach with a garden fork, and to head it

'Looking-for-Cornish-Pasties-on-the-Sheltered-Shore' left to do. It's incredible. It's only 6% of the final exam, but I am amazed that some of it seems to make sense. In fact, it's been amazing. After really committing it to God, he's just given me the go to drive at it all the time and what he's got me to write is brilliant.

Well, because of the project I haven't been doing too well in my other work. Last Wednesday I had revised for a timed essay I had to do for geography in the lesson, and I really did not do too well, at least, not as well as I hoped. I had to revise for a big chemistry test on Thursday and was behind in my project. I just got really het up in the evening and went for a Jambo Mungu walk to give it all to God. Well that evening in my notes I came across a section about someone who had 'wanted' Jesus and respect and popularity and stuff, as she was in the public eye. She realised that in fact she could only have Jesus by having him alone, or not at all. And God just showed me that although I'd say, 'Please help me in chemistry,' or whatever, really what I wanted was to do well so that I got an ego boost and I was pleased with myself. So I just committed my chemistry to him and told him that it would be to his glory and greatness and that I was doing it for him not me.

Next morning, I woke up, went to breakfast, and felt sick, so matron told me to lie on my bed all the morning. So, for only the second time since I've been at Tonbridge, I missed all my lessons, as I was ill, including the chemistry test. I had a good relaxing morning and then at 12 I felt a bit better, so I worked the whole of the afternoon and evening and got ahead on my biology. I saw the chemistry test paper on Friday, and I would not have done well. So that was a miracle, in fact even me getting depressed and finding that extract was a miracle as well.

On Saturday, Mr Saunders **[Pete's new housemaster]** read me my predictions made for the parents' evening. chemistry – C to E, biology – C to E, Geog – C/D (perhaps B). I could have died, but I said to God, 'Well it's all in your hands, so alleluia.' Mr Saunders said I should be worried, but I wasn't, it was wonderful. So what I need to do and what I would appreciate is prayer, and prayer that I can get down and do my work effectively. I mean, I am already working from 7 p.m.–11 p.m. in the evenings and all my free time, so please pray for this to be effective work. But it's so incredible that God's got it all in his hands. I was thinking that it's one thing to say, 'I'll stake my life on God' but to sincerely say, 'I'll allow God to let me do badly in my tests and exams' is something so different.'

In his journal he summarised:

Basically, it was a lot of work. I worked well, prayed well, grew as a Christian and God was very good to me in my exams.

Boy, it's now practically a year later and I'm supposed to remember all that occurred, from one year ago up to now. Help!

He often broke off in his journal to make asides like this. Once he was writing at Cairo airport when his plane was delayed there, similarly trying to remember the things that had happened a year before. But he did much better when writing his journal every day. Sometimes, with his dry sense of humour, he would actually write back to himself, or as if to his readers, as in the following:

> As it is, the holidays were all rather a long time ago, and no doubt some details may be omitted in the following account. I have no wish that this would cause any undue offence to any involved persons as there may be, but rather be regarded as a simple fault of my own mental capacity. I say this as I believe and feel that all events during my existence are of equal significance (almost) and the fact that some occurrences are more memorable to me than others is quite insignificant, contemplating the relative importance of these facts.
>   THAT'S A LOT OF KRUDE, PETE! [He added, in self-mockery.]

As we had promised, we arranged for Pete's cousin, who was a couple of years younger than him, to come out to stay for that summer holiday. It certainly gave Pete a new view on life. He writes, 'Well, during the holiday Steven came out to join me for the full eight weeks. That's a long time to be with someone I don't know too well. I prayed about it. It actually turned out to be great.'

Steve had no pretension about being a 'young guy' (as Pete put it) like his Tonbridge friends, but was free to laugh at kiddies and babies and was not ashamed to read some of our old children's books.

We were having a very busy time, so after a few days Julian dropped the two of them at the lakeside home of the Bunnys, for a self-catering break in their guesthouse (Dr Bunny and his wife Mary had retired from a Kenyan practice, and we had often camped with them). Pete commented:

We stayed there for a week in the end, courtesy of Kenyan politics (and riots) and it was actually one fantastic time: having hour-long teas with these wonderful colonials, also God-fearing old people (I mean that with much, much respect), sitting with them on the patio in front of the bougainvillaea, with the tea – 100% Kenyan, brought on a trolley with scones, cake and fresh Naivasha jam and butter. Not to forget the fresh cream and milk.

We had to cook our own supper on the fire outside. That was fun; it was Africa. Having hippo paddling about in the lake below, superb starlings everywhere. Umm, it was good.

We had two significant days when we left the place. The first, Diana Bunny [the artist daughter] a fantastic Memsahib, took us to a friend of hers, who was a plantation manager. We were shown all around their rose plantation and shown Sainsbury's Brussels sprouts, London asparagus. It was very interesting. There was a very London-type lad there who had some connection there for 6 weeks. He was very bored so we entertained him.

The other significant day was meant to be our last full day at Naivasha, the fourth day.

Pete had tried to take Steven into 'Hell's Gate', where
he, Colin and Jeff had had such fun the previous year.
They had no vehicle but planned to walk in. It was
quite a walk along that dust-filled road and it was hot.
When they got to the gate, to their surprise they found
the whole place had been changed and that now there
was a big entrance fee for the park. Neither had enough
cash, so they had to walk back in the heat of the day,
very discouraged.

The Bunnys felt very sorry for the forlorn pair, and
the next day, which was supposed to be their last
day, they rang up some friends of theirs who lived on
Crescent Island, an interesting half-submerged volcano
rim in the middle of the lake, and asked if the two of
them could come to visit the island. They lived at one
end of the island, and the rest had been made into a
private game ranch and reserve. Pete writes:

They were fine about it, so Diana drove Steve
and me down along the great Naivasha road that
was being repaired. Turning off this we drove
through one of the wazungu's [Europeans'] farms
to the lake. They bred polo horses – impressive
beasts. On arriving at Diana's friend's house we
greeted her and walked straight off. We ambled
round the island, through herds of wildebeest
and water buck; it was very um wonderful,
with some totally awesome views, plus a wicked
sunburn. On reaching the end of the island,
we sat down for lunch, and two kibokos [hippo]
swam in front of us. It was a good time.

However on arriving back at the house where
Diana was going to meet us, they told us of
the rioting in Nairobi and even Naivasha town.

That resulted in a long wait at the house while they drove off for some emergency potatoes, and also us staying at the Bunnys' for another two nights.

Our time at the cottage was great. As I said, we had to cook for ourselves in the dark for supper. We read many books and tried to sail Che Baringo [the reed boat we had bought at Lake Baringo].

They relaxed on the small lawn outside the guesthouse. It was on a slight rise, so you could look through the ancient thorn trees, across the floating islands of papyrus to the blue lake, and beyond to the darker blue hills on the far side. There were a pair of eagle owls nesting in those trees, and the whole place was alive with flitting birds of every colour. England and exams were far away, even the slight anxiety of wondering how his parents were coping with the riots in Nairobi.

It was here that Pete told Steve, 'My favourite verses are Romans 8:35-39 – "Who shall separate us from the love of Christ? Shall trouble or hardship or persecution or famine or nakedness or danger or sword? As it is written: 'For your sake we face death all day long; we are considered as sheep to be slaughtered.' No, in all these things we are more than conquerors through him who loved us. For I am convinced that neither death nor life, neither angels nor demons, neither the present nor the future, nor any powers, neither height nor depth, nor anything else in all creation, will be able to separate us from the love of God that is in Christ Jesus our Lord."'

Very comforting words, as he thought beyond the idyllic present to his return to school, the constant petty jeering of some of the boys, and even one very difficult member of staff. 'Dad eventually arrived to pick us up. We returned on a Wednesday and saw a burnt out bus from the riots, and many police. That was one of the best weeks I've had in many moons in Kenya.'

When they did get back home, they were immediately immersed, with an excited Colin, in preparations for the Harris family's arrival from Portugal for a week's visit. They took them to various places to see game and birds, including another memorable visit to Orus where they enjoyed a goat-roast. Pete wrote it all up in detail. 'I will never forget two images, one of sitting in one of the huts with the Pokot women and translating for Mama Jem; and the other, of the faces of Ma and Pa Harris saying goodbye to the Pokot lit up by the moon. Ni hajabu [out of this world, miraculous]!'

The rest of the holiday included the usual fun at Mombasa and some hard work from Pete on his geography project, taking photos and asking questions of the refugees who gathered almost daily in our garden now. Pete began to have a deep concern for the poor and underprivileged. Both he and Steven helped with the handing out of rations; at school the following year he would take on the thankless job of being the official school collector for charity. He was so successful in this that he won the special tie that was given when that job was done well. He only told me about it when I asked him about the tie. Characteristically, he never mentions it in his journal.

Pete went back to England full of enthusiasm to get things moving for God in the school.

21

'I Am Eighteen'

But first Pete had a week's geography field trip to contend with.

This was a difficult week really, trying to live with everyone, all with a completely different life style. But it had its good and amusing moments. Our field study centre was on the side of the river Severn, so I had some nice times of prayer and quiet lying by the river. We had an awful mama taking our group who had no idea how to control us. We exploited this to the full. We spent one day on the Welsh upland, theoretically studying soil; however we spent the greater part of the day chasing each other all over the gorse, etc., hurling soil samples at each other, jumping off cliffs and generally not paying the greatest attention to soil structure theory. A great day was a climb up Nant Ffrancon in Snowdonia country. That was a great walk on the last day.

Back at school at the beginning of the new term, Pete decided to start a new journal in which to write down what God was saying to him as he read his Bible each day. The original journal lingered on too, for a while, but was hopelessly out of date. He wrote a year later, 'Now I've left that school, I've little want to concentrate on it too much.'

The new journal begins, 'Having read the results that Esther [in the Bible] had from three days fasting, I have, for the first time, dedicated this weekend to God my Father and am fasting, apart from a snack tonight. The whole reason is that I just long to be used by God as his instrument of work.'

He had found some big commentaries at home. I wish he had asked me which ones to use. He started with William Temple and R.V.G. Taylor on John's Gospel. He struggled somewhat to record what he had learnt, and wrote frankly at the end, '(Not wholly understood). Boy, this is difficult stuff to follow but fascinating. I just want and need to repent of tonight, when I left this study and went to watch two lusty films, and enjoyed them, to an extent. Father how sinful can one be?'

Thank God, he does not judge us on our mistakes but looks at our heart and our 'run'. Do we want to follow him? Do we love him? Do we get up after a fall and start again in the great race that Paul calls it, looking to Jesus? God saw his heart and that he was beginning to have a longing to know God more.

After seeing some of his friends depressed, going through deep troubles like their parents' divorce, he writes:

'OH LORD, GIVE ME THE STRENGTH, WANT, LOVE AND WISDOM TO TAKE YOUR WORD TO THESE PEOPLE.'

God began giving him opportunities. One day a friend responded to something Pete said about Christianity, 'How can that be true? There is so much injustice in the world by birth.' The next day Pete wrote, 'Some friends started talking about sex before marriage. My Indian friends rattled some answers, then I got a say too. The joy I got from that was so [he added a drawing of a man with huge arms] big.' He was seeing the Lord opening up some remarkable conversations with other boys too, and he was probably doing more than he knew. One of his friends wrote later:

Pete was a very great encouragement to me in many ways. I am convinced he brought me my most important lessons at Tonbridge by showing me the importance of my faith and helping me to see there is so little time to accomplish so much.

Pete's encouragement to the Christian Fellowship was enormous and so much was achieved through his ideas and prayers.

He organised prayer sessions weekly with older members of the fellowship and many improvements and greater attendance has been shown through these.

It was Pete who also took the trouble to learn the guitar, to introduce music to the meetings. This added a crucial element of praise which was lacking in our weekly gathering. Pete was also very popular with everybody around the school, being so mild mannered, friendly and encouraging.

A staff member who was helping with the Christian Fellowship also longed to see the CF improve, and took the leaders, including Pete, to a day retreat. Pete thought, 'The guy said he really felt "there were blockages that needed to be moved" . . . apply to CF. My mind just flowed that I wanted to be able to do plays, preach, sing, worship; it all needs training. YWAM? Lord shall I go?' He decided to write off for the details of the YWAM (Youth With A Mission) discipleship course in Amsterdam. YWAM runs training schools for Christian work in many countries. I am not sure why Pete chose Amsterdam – I think friends had recommended it. The course in which he was interested was the Discipleship Training School (DTS) which conveniently started in September 1991, at the beginning of his gap year.

But now, he felt that he was in a battle. Some days, it seemed that God was not answering prayer. He wrote about a friend who had shown some interest in Christian things. The friend had said, 'I'm off the straight and narrow . . . on my way to hell.'

So I say, 'Right, God, I'm going to see him after CF committee,' praying that if God wants me to [speak to him] he'll be at his desk and ask me in. He's not even at his desk twice! Trying to get [someone from Holy Trinity Church, Brompton] on the phone to come to talk to CF, he's not in either. God, I don't know. I could think, 'What are you doing?' I want to serve you and I'm being stopped once I'm ready.

But no, because everything is to the best. Instead, you have it all in your hands. Praise God.

He added that, to top up his sorrows, a young Christian was drunk that evening, and Pete realised he had missed opportunities to speak out in his room to some boys who were talking about sleeping around with girls. But the next day he writes, rejoicing, 'And I thought God wasn't answering my prayers! In rugby, apart from getting a black eye, I'm in the 'fifths'. [He had been put back into the fifth school rugby team, something he had been praying for.] Coming back from that I knocked on [his friend's] window and he invited me in, as I had prayed last night. . . We talked about Jesus for a whole hour.'

So school was not all bad that term. He had been put in the rugby team as blind wing forward, which, he wrote to us, 'is really fun'. And later, 'School's great. I played rugby against Felstead yesterday in the 5th 15. It's great as we play good rugby but it's not too keen, so one doesn't feel as though you're playing only to be in the team.'

'Also,' he added, 'the fact that God's got all my work in his hands is so fantastic.' He also felt very positive about his geography project on the movement of refugees, but chemistry was still rather woeful. And, Pete wrote in a letter:

Chemistry really is bad. I find it difficult to concentrate for 80 minutes of confused chemical boredom. Geography project is great, as I said. If I do a good write-up the project subject is very good. I got a D in a geog. essay the other day, but so did everyone else so, that was not so bad . . . Looking over the text I knew it all and had only had bad examples, or not answered the question . . . Please pray for my work, and just that I will be constantly rejoicing in God.

He was still following his Thank-God-Whatever-Comes-If-I've-Done-My-Best course:

Yesterday was a chemistry block test, for which I had worked pretty hard, after an awful report previously. I expected to get 25-35/40 and sort of said, 'Lord be with me' and gave it to him only expecting a good mark. Today, I've found I got 17. So, what do I learn? - Don't get upset. I gave it to God and do still, even if not totally sincerely. He heard me. Therefore I only do what I can do for him: in this case, work, only expecting what I do to be to his glory not mine. '17/40 is your mark, Lord, not mine. To give the bad marks to you enables me (a bit more) to give you the good ones too.'

God allowed breaks for him in all the tensions of that term. Getting up to London to get to HTB – Holy Trinity Church, Brompton – with his sister always encouraged him, as did visiting her and his brother. Rozi had also taken him up to the Lake District at half-term, to visit a friend, which really encouraged his faith.

Now, late on 2nd December, he was having his usual Bible reading. He wrote in his Bible journal:

10 mins before my 18th birthday. I was thinking how I could remember it? What could I do better than spending it with God.

On Friday night I was unhappy/depressed about having to play rugby and have an artificial supper with Beneden Girls. I prayed, badly. But after being convinced that I would lose the game and hate it, it was 40-7 to us. Then the Beneden thing worked out well. I went out today to see Rozi, Uncle John and Gina, Jonny and Shaz and Rebecca and Jessica (Jonathan's new baby). HTB was SO good.

Munch called round with a card. God feels so real. If he answered those petty prayers, boy! My friend will become a Christian. Yes, sir!

I am 18 years old! Lord I commit this life, mine, to you. Humble it, keep it to you, and use it I pray. Alleluia!

The evil one would really put pressure on that commitment the following term.

22

1991: 'If You Do Not Stand Firm in Your Faith You Will Not Stand at All' (Isaiah 7:9)

Pete had a break back in Kenya over the holidays. He was the only member of the family who came that year, but we had the Foot family for a very entertaining Christmas Day, and in any case, he had plenty of work to do. At New Year he had only two days' break, high on a shelf of the Aberdare range of mountains.

He had time to read and study a book on prayer. He added at the end of his notes in the new journal:

> Father,
> I ask you for me to be supernaturally empowered to give a witness of the glory of the man, Christ Jesus and of his delivering power from all the oppression of Satan so that many unredeemed people might be made whole and then passionately filled with your perfect love for your beloved son and his dear church.

And the Lord knew this was the cry of Pete's heart.

Back in England he stayed with his sister, got to see a concert by the 'Fat and Frantic' music group, and helped to prepare a surprise party for Colin, who was in England for a few days from Portugal. Sadly, it made him late for school, and Mr Sanders, his housemaster, was not very happy about that.

Of that term Pete wrote:

This term is in fact a term I shall remember for a long time. I had managed to continue as a senior student, so had a small room out of the house. It was, in fact, tiny, long and thin; above a staff house. I remember the term being a very 'self' term. I would spend many evenings by myself in my very African/jazz orientated room crouching, at least working, over my desk, listening to jazz.

The mock A levels were four weeks into the term, so I worked as hard as I could for those. The term's significance really became noticeable about 1-2 weeks before those exams. Having applied to YWAM Amsterdam at the beginning of the term, I had committed six months to finding out more of God. However, at this time before the exams, I remember one Wednesday evening particularly, as I sat working over my chemistry/biology text books, being almost totally shocked as I realised I was questioning the actual existence of any God.

I would work at my desk, then fall onto my bed and then back to my desk, my revision notes often with questions like 'GOD?' written out on the page. I suppose one could say it was a pretty drastic time of my thinking/life so far.

Of all my thinking and rationalising, I can remember that the conclusion I came to was that there are two explanations to Pete Jackson. Either

I was God and everything existed inside of my mind, I didn't or at least couldn't exactly accept that, or there was a God of Trinity. I really feel there were a number of reasons for that, that it is or was one part of God's process in me, someday I'll fully, or more so, understand it. That's what I remember of the term.

It was an attack of the evil one on his mind to discourage him, but God gave him the grace to fight. Chemistry was not going too well either, but God sent encouragements to his beleaguered servant. He wrote in his prayer diary, 'Today I am told that the teacher has doubts of me getting a C even, in chemistry A level. Then, committing it to God, then working hard, I stopped and had my reading: "Stop trusting in man who has but a breath in his nostrils. Of what account is he?" (Isaiah 2:22) Wowee! Is that not great.'

And, later: 'I handed in my chemistry paper today, to God's glory. It worked!'

His fears would suddenly come back. 'Is God a figment of my imagination? . . . I've come to know again that he is real, and I believe more than before, with some relapses.' It was just as well, for his faith was certainly tested the following week with his chemistry mocks.

Just want to give it to God, with no worry involved, because I could do very badly. I pray it's to his glory.

I did do very badly. Praise GOD. Well I now know there is one God.

Tonight: 'If you do not stand firm in your faith, you will not stand at all.' (Isaiah 7:9)

He came out to Kenya for Easter, his last school holidays, and of course, his studies loomed large. His 'mock' results had been E, C, C – both Cs being 3% below a B.

However, those still weren't going to get me to where I wished to go. I think by that time I had chosen Leeds as my first choice, Birmingham my second. So I decided to work again as hard as I could. I aimed at 8 hours a day and in the first week achieved about 6–7, which wasn't too bad. Having realised my chemistry notes were atrocious, as were much of my biology, and with ambitious ideas of map making, I set about a colourful noting of my text books and notes. The family were due to fly to Mombasa on Saturday. Being such a disciplined boy . . . I declined the invite in the hope to work an extra week.

We were most impressed with what he was doing, and went off to the coast rather sad, but proud of him for wanting to work. It was a time of political unrest in the Middle East and possible increase in hijacking, so tourists were avoiding travelling to Kenya that spring. Therefore all the hotels were charging rock-bottom prices to tempt residents to use them.

It was also the end of another era. We felt that God was telling us to return to England, after nearly forty years in Africa. So, knowing that it would be our last holiday together as a family in Kenya, we decided to go to all the places we could usually never afford to visit. After going to Watumu on the coast, we were returning to Nairobi and then making off for some other wonderful hotels up-country. Pete felt the coast was the one he least wanted to miss out on to do his extra work. It turned out to be another special time with God.

There was a week before we all left. He wrote in his Bible journal:

Back Home in Kenya 17th March '91
I am happy. I'm at home. Coming back here, doubt about God seems to dissolve away. I'm reading C.S. Lewis's book Mere Christianity at the moment, which is a blessing.

Well, having just sunbathed/prayed instead of going to Ziwani church, and praying for CF, etc. I ask God to guide me as to what I should now read and I open up to Haggai (as it is short) and it's about God telling Israel to rebuild the temple. CF!

On Monday, he was back reading Isaiah again and the verse that struck him again was *'If you do not stand firm in your faith, you will not stand at all'*. He wrote it down again on the Wednesday and commented:

Yesterday I was thinking, as there is this real God, I want to give him everything, and how can I? Last night, getting into bed (the top bunk), again I thought I heard that, if I so wish to give everything, I need to begin . . . trusting you completely for:
• YWAM dosh
• safety next week [He would be all alone in our bungalow in Nairobi except for the dog and James out in his bedsit.]
• A levels

So Saturday came, and we all left for the airport. Pete wrote, 'Everyone has left for the coast. I have an evening to concentrate on God. I am realising that as God is who he is, he is so great – so great it is hard to accept.' He quoted from Paul Yonggi Cho's book *Prayer: Key to Revival:*[7]

> One of the greatest lies of Satan is that we just don't have time to pray. However, all of us have enough time to eat, sleep and breathe. As soon as we realise that prayer is as important as sleeping, eating, breathing, we will be amazed at how much more time will be available to us for prayer . . . I believe the same level of revival can be experienced in your church . . . The answer is prayer.

The next morning he had been invited to lunch by Julian's assistant, Catherine Garton. He walked over to the Pentecostal church and, arriving early, sat outside. 'I began to tell God all my problems with him. I remember finding the service pretty significant.' He added 'A memorable day.'

On Tuesday the Lord encouraged him, through his reading, concerning the arduous timetable he had given himself. He writes, 'One prominent verse, as I try and work and it is raining, is: "Be strong . . . and work. For I am with you."'

And he did work well that week. We were very glad to see him on the Thursday and take him off with us on the Thursday afternoon to Lake Naivasha Hotel, on the start of our posh week! From there, the family rushed off to watch the great annual Car Rally Safari for the last time. We were home for Sunday, but on Monday morning they were again out early to the last Safari checkpoint to see the first cars in. Pete says, 'Jonny, Colin and I rushed out to the Thika road to the Utalii College and, exploiting our skin tone and JJ's video camera, walked straight into the final enclosure for the Safari Rally. Standing right with the reporters as they interviewed the world's top rally drivers. It was a very good time.'

God was very good to us that week. We went to Tree Tops that night, a copy of the hotel where Princess Elizabeth had been spending the night when she heard that her father had died and that she had become Queen. We had never been before, so it was fun, especially the extra embellishments for tourists. Then we went north into the scrub land of Samburu country, bordering on to Pokot. Pete told me, 'Mum, I'm coming back here. I want to explore all those hills.' I remember thinking, 'I wonder what the boy will do; I hope he won't waste his life exploring.'

We had a great week. Then Pete was back studying again, but still taking time to be with God each day. He wrote one day, 'I really tried to depend on God's strength, not mine. It worked.' His last prayer entry in his journal that holiday was:

Father,
I pray that I will work in your strength, not mine. I ask that the work, then exams will be to your glory.
   God, I pray that I may find the correct balance between your exams and your Christian/CF work in the term.
   I pray so much that you will release CF from its 'Public School' spiritual position. WAKE IT UP!
   I ask whether the Bible study is right, and bless it if it is.

Lord, I pray for YWAM. Direct me where to get prayer and money support from.

As the term got going, God answered Pete's prayer in a remarkable way. One Friday evening Warren Watson, a great friend of Colin's, was invited (at Pete's instigation) to speak to the Christian Fellowship. Warren later wrote:

> I hadn't seen Pete for a couple of years . . . He had grown tall and filled out and now was such a handsome young man, confident, yet with an underlying gentleness and quietness about him. The subject of my talk was Christian commitment. I shared my own testimony of how Jesus had transformed me from drug addiction/alcoholism into a follower and then explained the gospel. There were approximately 20 to 25 boys present, plus one master. After my talk I felt it was right to ask anyone to stand up if they really wanted to follow Jesus and live completely all out for him. After I gave the invitation, no one stood. I had just sung a song about being ready to meet Jesus when he returned, so I felt it important to repeat the challenge to the boys about making sure that they would be ready. Pete stood. He was the only one who stood up in the room. It took a lot of courage, especially in front of all his peers. But then, to my surprise, one by one, every boy in the room stood up, including the master present. They stood together, united in their choice to follow Jesus and live for him and then to meet him.
>
> Every time I think of that, I always remember Pete standing, then looking around the room at everyone. And then all those boys standing. I talked later to Pete and he told me that there were a small number who had never taken a public stand for Jesus before.

Pete characteristically, never even mentions this in his journal.

But there was another surprise and answer to prayer for him. The headmaster had allowed him and Ian Sheppard, the secretary of the Christian Fellowship, to invite a team from Holy Trinity Brompton to come and speak at one of the Sunday services. Each Sunday, at the school, one of the chapel services was compulsory, the other voluntary; the team was to speak at the voluntary service, which fell that week in the evening. Then the headmaster had changed it to the morning service, which was always much better attended. Ian and Pete were tremendously encouraged.

Pete cried daily to God for the school, but advertising this meeting was a problem when you only saw the boys in your own house and the few who were in your teaching set. But he wrote:

> I praise God for Ian's and my opportunity to speak in chapel (to advertise the special service). Take away our pride, and work in these people. Get them to the service . . . please. Then blow their minds . . . please.
>
> 1 Peter 3:12, 'For the eyes of the Lord are upon the righteous and his ears are attentive to their prayer"!
>
> Lord, we have been praying so much for the meeting, etc., etc. . . . Lord, please can we be righteous so that your ears can be attentive to our prayer.

He was praying for his friends who scoffed at God, who went out and got drunk; and that weak Christians would not get drawn away by the scoffers. His daily reading was now from 1 Peter. He wrote:

> 1 Peter 3:21
> This is the strongest argument and probably

most correct for becoming baptised. However, I do well remember standing up at Spring Harvest at 14 and dedicating my life to God. Today, I consider my personal baptism, my commitment to God. Lord, I want to renew that.

Lord Jesus, I feel my spirit is becoming proud in wee ways, from how you have used me in this HTB thing.

Lord, PLEASE, no. Forgive me, humble me, and give me the correct attitude – one, I suppose, in which I am just joyful in the privilege. Yes Sir!

He read through his journal on the Saturday before Simon Downham, a barrister friend, came with his team from Holy Trinity. He saw how, sadly, two boys he had prayed much for had made commitments then backslidden. He prayed:

Tomorrow Simon and co. come to a God-organised service. He believes, God, you are going to do something great. My faith is a pittance. Yet I have prayed, God does answer prayer, and most of all I pray my inadequacies will not be a barrier between you and me and your work. . . . Lord please work tomorrow and give me faith now. Please, please, please.

I pray Lord you will wash this school with holiness. It's Pentecost day tomorrow. Wash it also with yourself. Please.

One boy from Judde remembered Pete taking him for 'prayer walks' round the school, which had a profound influence on him at that time.

The great day came and, to their amazement, hundreds of boys streamed into the chapel. Pete does not describe what happened nor if he heard of any direct results but he just wrote in his journal, 'ALLELLUIA, IN THE LIGHT OF GOD'S REALITY. AMEN!'

Sadly I have lost his letters for the rest of term, but Ian Sheppard wrote, 'It was [Pete's] insistence that we addressed chapel . . . We both trusted the situation to God and he took care of it. It was this example of Pete's total confidence in God for help that so affected me and was a great challenge.'

At the time, I think Pete had some backlash. 'Today has been good. I've thought of my God much more,' he wrote the next day, and he quotes several verses from 1 Peter on suffering; maybe some boys teased him after that service.

The next hurdle looming was his exams. Academic work had continued to dominate his thoughts and prayers all term.

The battle of me, realism and God continued, combined with that of the work load. Karl came to UK to earn. It was good to see the guy and to go to stay with him for a bit. I remember just counting down the months, weeks, days to A levels. I had no idea how I would do. Chemistry, I would work my butt at, and get 30-40% in tests. In geography, my essays rose to A-B, then fell to C-B; the last test result I got back in biology was about 37%. Trog had said 60% should be our minimum . . . So it was a sort of anxious time. I really did put effort into my faith in the Lord though. I know it was pretty shallow, but a lot of my work I would pray over. Even in my weakness, God, my Lord, my Saviour, Friend and Father used this.

On the Tuesday, before the exams started, he hurriedly read chapter 5 of 1 Peter.

I've just read this passage, twice. I go through it again slowly and find this verse which I had not seen before. Man!

'Cast all your anxiety on him because he cares for you' (1 Peter 5:7).

Today is the day I've felt most concerned, very definitely, about – my dear exams. And I get this. Wow!

Lord, help me to cast my anxiety, even more to know this is directly from you, today, this minute. Proof that there is this relationship.

Looking at some old chemistry papers a few days later, again that stomach-gripping feeling came over him.

I get kinda worried uh . . . uh . . . BUT. My GOD says:
- 'Let us then approach the throne of grace with confidence, so that we may receive mercy and find grace to help us in our time of need' (Hebrews 4:16).
- 'Cast all your anxiety on him because he cares for you' (1 Peter 5:7).
- 'Trust and obey, for there is no other way . . .'
- 'That your faith . . . may be proved genuine' (1 Peter 1:7).

God's perfect plan for moi.

The 3rd June arrived.

> Just before going into my chemistry exam
> today, I opened Psalms, praying and got . . .
> 'Lord, you have assigned me my portion . . .
> surely I have a delightful inheritance' (Psalm
> 16:5–6).
>   Then Psalm 18:2, 'The Lord is my rock, my
> fortress and my deliverer.'
>   W.O.W.

The weight of exams brought their reaction.

> Wed 12th June
> Realising I'm in another low now and trying
> to pray my way up/out – at least to give it to
> God.

> Saturday
> Through prayer and concentration my
> realisation of God is slowly rising again. Boy,
> do we have to be dedicated to stay wise.

The results that he saw from the HTB meeting were
a new fervour and joy in the CF group, which was a
great encouragement to him. He doesn't mention many
names or numbers, but significantly copied out 2 Peter
3:8–9: *'With the Lord a day is like a thousand years, and
a thousand years are like a day. The Lord is not slow in
keeping his promises.'*

> At CF today, there was a beginning of a change.
> Lord I really pray that this thing will change
> to something that is good to your glory . . . CF

was brilliant yesterday. It was beginning to be alive. Lord, please keep it like that + better.

And there definitely were other results, even if they were not instantly apparent. A mother wrote to us two years later:

> We want to thank you for what [Pete] has done for our two boys through his great enthusiasm. It appears he brought new life and ideas to the CF at Tonbridge. Our younger son says but for this, and the fact that Pete talked to him and encouraged him, he would certainly have ceased to attend . . . Two other parents, unknown to each other, both said to me what I myself had been thinking – 'Pete has sown seeds.' We all share the same faith that these seeds will blossom.

And a friend of Pete's wrote:

> I knew Pete principally from the CCF [Navy Corps] activities in which we both participated. We spent many amusing (and some not so amusing) hours with each other . . . plodding round the Brecon Beacons or attempting to windsurf around Bough Beech reservoir. His enthusiasm and untiring energy for these and other activities were a fine example to many, and there are few people that I know who showed as much enjoyment for life as Pete did . . . I was something of a pseudo Christian. I believed in God when the time suited me. Hearing the news of Pete's death gave me serious doubts about my half belief . . . [It was] . . . an important factor in my desire to seriously look for the first time, for the truth. . . . Other friends have thought about their lives, and it has helped me to look for, and by progression, to discover that God really exists. I committed my life to him and he has filled me with an extraordinary joy and sense of peace.

What joy that would have given Pete.

Karl's visit earlier had also reminded them of their
great plan for their 'gap' year. When Karl had called
back to visit his friends at the school, he wrote:

> It was lunchtime. The grounds were put to sleep by a
> rhythmic hymn heard from a distance. It grew louder and
> less harmonised as I approached Judde House. I carefully
> crossed the treacherous windy road and confronted my
> old brick boarding house. It was consumed by thick green
> vines, and had the same old, heavy door, which I was
> convinced was purposely in place to hinder any fleeing
> fugitive and allow for easy recapture. I went in and heard
> that familiar lunch riot which occurred every afternoon
> instantly following Grace. My nose led the way towards
> the smell of beef gravy and baked potatoes. Moments
> after I entered the crowded fiesta, I was swallowed up
> by a table of hoodlums I had once called roommates.
>
> We talked through the night. Pete had not changed. He
> was still a sloppy mess, wearing a ripped and faded lime
> green sweater which I believe he had owned since birth.
> His reddish straw hair remained self-cut and uncombed,
> and he still had dreams of helping the needy and saving
> the world. He was liked and respected by teachers and
> classmates and no one questioned his dreams . . .
>
> I was let in on some disturbing news. Pete had decided
> to begin his dream of helping the needy. He was going
> to spend his whole gap year as a volunteer missionary,
> touring the world and helping anyone from AIDS patients,
> to drug addicts, to hunger-struck tribes. I'll admit that he
> was not being selfish, but it sure put a damper on our
> plans.

Pete was sad to disappoint them. Karl and Rupert did
the Canada tour without him, but Pete himself was
quite sure by now that God wanted him to attend the

YWAM discipleship course in September in Amsterdam. He then planned to work in Kenya as a volunteer with the Africa Inland Mission with about a dozen other 'gap year' young people until August. As someone has written, he knew he was being called 'by a different drum'.

Towards the end of term he wrote:

One of my best passages:
'After this, Jesus went out and saw a tax collector by the name of Levi sitting at his tax booth. "Follow me," Jesus said to him, and Levi got up, left everything and followed him' (Luke 5:27–28).

Rozi and Jonathan in Turi uniform, with Pete, Colin and Annabel the Labrador

Pete in his Kenyan sun hat, aged 4

Pete in his rugger kit with his certificate, at Turi

Pete with Peter Kanyi's sons in the sitting room in Nairobi

Beside the river in Tsavo East

Colin, Jonathan, Masai herd boy who joined the picnic,
Pete, Rozi, Julian and Rachel on the Ngong Hills, Nairobi

Pushing the Combi through a dry river bed in Samburu,
April 1991

Julian, Jonathan, Colin and Pete at Lake Bogoria (Hannington) in the Rift Valley, April 1991

The family at lunch in Mtito Andei, halfway to Mombasa

23

'Our God Is An Awesome God'

So now the ten blissful weeks of time at home stretched before Pete, though he was sad to think that these would be our last August holidays in Kenya. Not that it would be a holiday for Julian and me. Our plans had had to be altered; now we would not be able to leave until the following spring, as there was no one available until then to take up the refugee work. Our packing was going very slowly because we were still involved in work. There were still many refugees coming every week to our garden, hoping for some help to survive. They came for food, and Pete was a great help in the distribution. And they still came for Bible study. Pete often led one of the small groups.

I can see him now, cross-legged on the grass. I always took a stool for myself when I was leading, but the refugees themselves generally preferred to sit on mats. Pete liked to be on the ground with them. He had compassion on them and they knew it. Years later a woman who had been in Bible studies he had taken, and who had also helped in our house on occasions, told me 'Mum, I cannot tell you how miserable I was last year. You were out of the country and I was working for someone but they would not believe how ill I was, or, what very bad financial troubles I was in. I slept badly as I was in great pain, but I dreamt one night. I dreamt that Pete came to me [he was then in heaven] and said in his kind voice, 'Mary, it will be all right.' I woke up so encouraged and knew God was remembering me. That day someone gave me three pairs of shoes, and shortly afterwards I was sent to hospital and recovered.'

It is significant that the first verses Pete copied into his Bible journal that holiday were:

'I tell you, my friends, do not be afraid of those who kill the body and after that can do no more. But I will show you whom you should fear: Fear him who, after the killing of the body, has power to throw you into hell' (Luke 12:4).

It's about depending on God for everything. 'But seek his kingdom, and these things will be given to you as well' (12:31).

It ends with this verse: 'From everyone who has been given much, much will be demanded' (12:48).

Moi. The Lord has given me too much; all I can give is my life. This is what I want to do, completely.

And later, as he was reading Proverbs, he comments:

Solomon warns against fleshly uncleanness. [He had been struggling with friends talking about girls and his feelings about them, which he found that with prayer God helped him with.] Temptations are so strong but the results so destructive that Solomon repeats it many times. It has been

Satan's way to draw people away into idolatry and other religions. We are warned not to approach even the borders of sin. If we thrust ourselves into temptation, we mock God when we pray.

In Proverbs 5 it says 'Drink water from your own cistern, running water from your own well.' Although this in context refers to being faithful to one's wife, I really felt that it also applies to one's cistern being one's own spirit/soul and character. At this time when I am leaving the shelter of public school, even home, it is all the more important that I do take all my actions/words from my soul – not others – which is the beginning of a God-influenced soul.

As we knew how weary-minded he must be, we wanted to be sure he had a good holiday before going to the Youth With A Mission training course in the autumn. As we could not stop to go on holiday ourselves, we decided to send Pete off with Rozi to the coast.

Rozi had been living at home. She had very lovingly given up a good job in London and had come to Kenya to work and help us pack the belongings collected during our twenty years in Nairobi (though Pete described it as 'helping Mum, theoretically, to pack, but practically, with the refugees!'). They went off on the train together. Pete remembered the journey down on the train, 'Stayed up late talking to a traveller kid with Rozi, who had a really sound 'Christo' talk with the guy. Also remember a girl telling me my sister wanted me in the toilet . . . found her stooping over the wet, muddy floor of the choo variant, rather frantic, having lost her contact lens. Sisters! We finally found it, which was actually really Mungu [God], in her wash bag.'

The train journey to the coast is an experience in itself. You travel overnight. The train lurches from station to station, rattling as it gathers speed. The second class carriages are the corridor type with rooms off the corridor that you have to book in advance. There are four beds to each compartment. You can rent your bedding on the train; the steward brings you a bundle of blankets, a pillow and crisp white ironed sheets. The toilets are mostly the Asian variety, sunk in the floor. There is an interesting restaurant where supper and full breakfast are served. The supper menu is always the same: Pete wrote, 'I can't eat chicken curry now without thinking of the KR trains and leaking choos, but the journey was good.'

They had a great time in Watamu together just resting, swimming and pottering round the shops. When I asked Pete what they did, weeks later, he said, 'The thing I remember most was the song that Rozi hummed or sang everywhere':

> Our God is an awesome God.
> He reigns from heaven above,
> With wisdom, power and love.
> Our God is an awesome God!
> ('Our God is an Awesome God' by Rich Mullins)

He was also to learn from Rozi that 'God is no man's debtor'. She headed back to England where jobs were scarce. Several of her college friends had been made redundant, and yet, she was offered two good places within a week!

One day there was a telephone call for Pete. Afterwards, he came to the room where I was packing trunks, with his face shining and slightly pink.

'Mum. That was Mr Sanders.'

'No! Quick! What did he say!'

'He rang from school because – I can't believe it – but I did best in the whole of Judde for my exams. I've got C for chemistry and As for biology and geography. Truly God is good!'

We dropped everything and went out for a meal to celebrate!

The time was coming for him to go to Holland for the YWAM course. Julian encouraged him to send out a circular letter to several of our friends who prayed regularly for us, so that they could pray specifically for him.

Pete was a normal boy with normal hormones. Several times that holiday he mentioned in his journal that if people were talking about girls he had uncomfortable feelings afterwards. He prayed about it and felt that it was wrong, for him, to have these feelings, and he praised God for delivering him from them. But he was aware of the problem, so he mentioned it in his first prayer circular.

This is an opportunity for which I am extremely thankful, and a time which I am much looking forward to. However, I do not feel that I should take this time lightly . . . My first request is, therefore, for prayer that God will be able to effectively teach me through this to serve him then, and in future, to the extent that I will not waste lessons and lose concentration, etc., but will constantly be hearing from God.

Many people have also said that Amsterdam is a tough place. The school where I shall be living is I believe near the infamous red-light district of Amsterdam. As this is an area where Satan has worked to his full to destroy God's creation of humanity, and an area full of evil, prayer for protection against this and strength and wisdom to deal with all situations, in God's grace, would be tremendously appreciated.

Several people replied and this was a big encouragement to him.

Two outings before he left Kenya were very significant, for God used them to help his faith to grow – rather like David's experiences in the Bible with the lion and the bear!

One was in the company of Chris Foot. At school they had planned to hire a car and head up to the desert of north Kenya, but when they looked into it they found that hiring a vehicle was not a cheap matter, especially when five of them planned to go. So they decided to go in the Foots' small, open Datsun pick-up. 'The decision,' Pete wryly commented, 'saved me/us money, but not the owner.' In fact if we had known their plans, I think we would have vetoed it.

They had 2 trunks, 4 jerry cans, 2 spare wheels, 5 pack sacks, 2 tents, 1 large bag of vegetables, 4 camp chairs, 1 camp table, spade, bucket, water containers, tarpaulins and 1 large cotton-stuffed mattress – all tied on in various places, as well as three folk and all their personal luggage in the back. They were to travel on a road dangerous for dust, potholes and the like, in 'this 1600cc, two-wheel drive pick-up = ambitious', as Pete wrote. They did string up oars and wire as a

frame to put a cover on, in case of rain! They hoped
to get up into Northern Frontier and back in about six
days, because Pete wanted to get back for the wedding
of Art Davis's daughter. They started off cheerfully but
exhausted – because of packing they had not got to
sleep until 3 a.m., and had to start out at 6.15 a.m.!

Their aim was to get up into the desert as soon as
possible. They passed the turning to Orus the first day
and travelled on past Maralel to the north without
incident, except for stopping for stores and camping for
the night. The second day they only planned a short trip
on this punishing road, when they saw a Land Rover
in the ditch with some children standing by it. It had
rolled over; mercifully no one was seriously injured.
Chris insisted they go straight back to the nearest
town to report it to the police who would get help for
them. Pete wrote, 'It made us more conscious that
we were kinda vulnerable in the back, but we
drove on.'

Shortly afterwards, they ploughed into a sandbank.
Then the fun began – their fan belt was broken and
they overheated every few miles. The next few days
were a series of catastrophes and God-incidences; the
right person coming to help at the right time; Pete and
Roger – Chris's South African friend – moving rocks
off the track in front of the truck in fierce heat as Chris
eased her slowly forward; hours spent bent over the
engine, trying to fix up fan belts from camera straps or
rubber strip. Roger remembers Pete's friendly manner,
using his scant Swahili to talk to people of every
culture on the road, then, finally, after they had had
some repairs done, singing in the back of that truck for
mile after mile, all the songs about heaven they could
think of. I think it was memories of that that made
Chris phone with the message, 'He got there before us,'

the following year. They could so easily have all been there that week!

Pete made two interesting comments later in his journal about his reading from Proverbs 10:

> 'The lips of the righteous nourish many' (v.21).
>
> The first verse today when I'm feeling a dummy after entertaining Chris and 2 friends badly yesterday. 'Nourish many'. I've been praying that Christ will enable me to be confident and talk well with people. The most successful conversations are where people are actually nourished; it is 'the lips of the righteous' that do this. Lord, make me righteous, so that you may nourish many.

And later:

> We must not look for praise from men, but from GOD. Lord, as I begin to wallow into this 18+-year-old life, what a vital message this is to be. How I must with all dudes and girls associate, not as a struggling-to-be-cool self, but a representative of who? . . . of the Lord.

Then, just the week before he had to fly off to England en route for Amsterdam, two of Pete's cousins decided to try to climb Mount Kenya; something Pete had often longed to do. We stocked him up with chocolate and dried fruit and vegetables – which was fortunate, because they ran out of food on the trip – and waved goodbye to the three of them. Thankfully, they were driving a Land Rover this time. Three days later we were back in the car park waiting for their return. The vehicle chugged in, covered with mud, and a very grubby but radiant Pete emerged.

'What was it like Pete?'

'It was awesome, Mum. Just awesome,' he replied, joy shining through the dust on his face.

24

YWAM: 'I Don't Want to Miss Out on His Plan'

After that memorable holiday, Pete flew back to England to pack for Amsterdam.

He was now reading Ezra in his time with God. He comments:

> Reading today of the returned Israelites putting up the temple + altar. What do I learn from them?
>   1. It was their priority; the first thing they did.
>   2. They put their all into it; it was expensive and it took all their time.
>   3. They made it good quality – cedars from Lebanon.
>   4. They continued, even when threatened.
>   5. They gave God all the glory for the opportunity and depended on his love.
> As I proceed to build God's temple – myself – I pray these qualities will be in my plans.

He was excited, yet apprehensive about going to the YWAM course, but was also amazed at the things God was doing for him. He wrote to us:

I'm not quite in Amsterdam . . . I'm presently
sitting on a train which is apparently going
to Dover. Wow! . . . People have been very
generous giving bits of money here and there,
so I have survived well. [His last host] was also
very generous in help to YWAM, although I
can't pretend that I didn't pray that he would
be!

Although Pete had seen God provide amazingly with
his finances for his parents and family, it was very
faith-strengthening to see God do it for him.

He later wrote about his arrival:

I got to Amsterdam station plus pack, bag and
guitar – all very heavy. Survived the struggle
onto the bus, walked into a reception where
all had American accents . . . I had arrived.
I dumped my bags in my room (I'm sharing
with an American for two weeks then we go to
singles) and talked to people as I ate supper.
Here I got invited to a concert in some club by
a YWAM group going into nightclubs. I went,
getting back for my first night's sleep at 3
a.m.

On the second day, a Sunday, there was a reception
for the new students in the evening. Jim Isom, one
of the lecturers, who was Pete's group leader, later
wrote:

I remember Pete on that first day at YWAM . . . As he
entered the stage room for our student reception, his smile,
easy friendly manner and carroty red hair announced his
presence without a word. Despite his noticeable English

reserve and 'formal' British accent, it seemed he was known and loved by everybody before the evening meal was out. At 18, Pete was everyone's son or brother.

In his second letter, Pete described some of the activities he had already done in the orientation period: visiting the YWAM centres such as The Ark, a home for outcasts, and The Cleft, a cafe in the red-light district.

I mean, in no way can I write all my feelings, etc. . . . Meeting people with such a heart for God's work and really feeling God's victory, like right in the middle of the red-light district. Wow! That was pretty amazing . . . I really feel I'm being shown how much one can get involved. God really was trying to show me that I can't be a super Christian, etc. but must really depend on his strength, and trust him. That is what I pray for.

He was back studying Isaiah again. He was noticing that Moab suffered so much because of her pride. He wrote, 'Pride. Father, I pray for protection from it.'

The YWAM course consisted of this week of introduction, eleven weeks of lectures and practical work in Amsterdam and then a further outreach, outside Holland, to give them a cross-cultural vision and to apply all the theory they had been learning. It was also intended to teach them something of team dynamics, and to raise up leaders from among the students; as well, of course, as helping the groups of Christians with whom they would be involved. They could choose which outreach to go on. That year the destinations included Russia, India and Hungary, so there was not much time to get bored.

First then, he had to choose the practical work in Amsterdam that he would be involved with. He wrote in his third letter:

> The time so far has been wonderful . . . I look forward very much to our city outreach whilst in Amsterdam. I signed up this morning to work with evangelical (evangelistic) groups with students living in horrific high-rise buildings, and waking at 4.30 a.m. once or twice a week to walk round and invite drug addicts, etc. on the street to a breakfast and befriend them.

To comfort his parents he added, 'They ensure we're with experienced people, at least to begin with.'

He decided that trying to keep up his old journal – by now a whole year out of date – as well as his prayer journal was not possible as they were too interwoven, so he decided to keep just one diary. Rather whimsically, he noted:

> I feel I should record what I learn in lessons as well as in the Bible. Learnt today that our heavenly body is always up [he drew a cheerful stick man here with his arms in the air!] and our earthly one sometimes down with earth life. Trying to join these together is a process, a way that God works.
>
> It is this process which, God, I pray you will work in me.

Jim Isom had recommended that they record honestly everything that they thought God was telling them.

From then on, Pete worked at this. He wrote to us:

I am now sitting at a very comfy desk in my single room. I'm much enjoying its privacy. Mum and Dad, this time is being so wholesome and fantastic. I last wrote after the first week of orientation, so really the beginning. The last two weeks now have really got us into the teaching, though the lectures seem to be only about 50% of the learning in a day, as so many other things happen throughout the day that I'm always involved with activities here and there.

Anyway, the lectures have been really great, the first section of which being on the 'Exchanged Life of Christ' . . . basically the idea of 'Christ in you, the hope of glory' as we allow God to work through us. I've found that I've done a lot of learning, and now am praying and seeing God beginning this process in us as 'we surrender ourselves to transparency' . . . yes. I'm trying to get used to American phraseology, etc. . . . It does amuse moi! Basically, that was good and led by a visiting speaker. I don't think I mentioned that it is all translated into Dutch! At least they say it's Dutch . . . I find the slower pace helps me think, so it's v. good.

This last week has been focused on – phraseology again – 'dysfunctional and functional' families, which apparently means 'family hurts'. It has really been a wonderful teaching. I've been in tears all week about my disrupted childhood! No, but seriously it is wonderful to see God directly working in others who have had traumatic childhoods, have hatred, etc. . . . I mean it's sometimes hard to understand it all, but like one wonderful Australian guy said, 'Pete, I've never cried so much in my life.'

And then, among all this is worship and people having words of knowledge, etc.; two of these being directly for me, has been quite a thing. The lectures finish at 12.30 p.m. We have lunch, an afternoon which is 'free' but is spent talking, then going over notes. Supper is at 5.30, and the evening (if off) has been spent talking, though now is taken up with involvement in various ministries around Amsterdam. These have been and will be a significant part of this time . . .

What have I done already? Last Tuesday morning was really my first time out. At 6 a.m. we walked through a section of the red-light district, giving coffee out to anybody who was around at that time. Not so many were tourists! It was a very, not good, but 'striking' time, Boy! Do I feel your prayers for protection against Satan. Others go into here and immediately get really depressed, etc. Although recognising a tremendous need there, I have felt no attacks like this as yet, no lust, etc., so I am really thankful to God and for your prayers!!!! The first time we walked through the red-light district, I didn't make a conscious effort to not look around, only talked to others in the group and, boy, I cannot remember a single unclean thing from the time there!

My main work, though, is going to be with the students in the very depressing housing block area and prayer to be able to befriend these would be most appreciated.

Three years later, we heard that a regular meeting that Pete helped to start with the students and the local pastor called 'Eat and Meet the Dutch' was still a very popular evening, attracting up to 120 students.

Did I mention that our talks about the holiness of rock music have some evidence, or whatever, here? One ministry is to the young in the city. A YWAM night club (The Steiger) on a boat holds Rock and Roll Bible studies on Wednesdays which are v. good. Talking to the guys here, they are some of the most 'on fire' guys I have ever met and their soundness is not in question. I mean God is using their ministry. The club's official group 'No Longer Music' is presently on a huge tour of USSR, which Vineyard, Southern Baptists and YWAM are all participating in. So . . . Anyway, Friday night the ministry goes into nightclubs around Amsterdam and invites/witnesses, etc. I really felt I should go. So Friday night (Mum's face!) we met at the boat and prayed for about an hour. 20 of us then set off. I, in fact, felt I should go on a prayer walk round a square there. We never made it to the square, but ended up witnessing to people on the way. A real time of learning and needing to have the strength of God for confidence, etc. Very good.

So many other things . . . O boy, so much to write!

I will say, please pray that God will show me which outreach to go on, that's important.

Also that all spiritual growth will be really concrete, nothing super-spiritual, but one solid foundation to stand on when I leave here.

With the Steiger team, he also helped with speaking in schools on a weekend mission. A friend wrote:

His favourite word was 'Right!' He would give the English lesson on the word 'Awesome' by writing down four definitions on the board and having the Dutch students guess the meaning. Pete loved to share the meaning of the word awesome, because it is such a good word to describe God. I guess the greatest way he shared that message was in the huge enthusiasm with which he shared. And that lasts longer than words spoken.

Being transparent had interesting results in his journal. He had mentioned his thoughts before, but now he was more explicit. It was a period remarkable in several ways.

It was a time when he was full of questions

'God are you real?' [He drew a man being pounded with thoughts.] 'Is this me? Is God just a figment of my imagination?'

'If you are real, do you really want a relationship with me?'

'What happens when someone who is not a believer asks you for things?'

'What are God's motives in caring for me?'

'How can I be used by God like Peter/Paul was?'

'What do I do with feeling fragile over what others think of me?'

'Why do I have these questions/doubts?'

And yet, that God should choose to begin to teach this to me I consider an awesome privilege. He's so radical, so opposite to what the world says.

I ask you to reveal and teach these realities to me, because I need you to, so I can present them as truth at university.

A thought comes into my head that hearing so much of this means I may become brainwashed. This is a thinking from English culture.

In the goodness of God, he had now chosen to study the book of Acts in his private reading each day. Here he found, to his joy, many of the answers to his questions.

It was a time of deep learning
He was learning many things. Here are some of the themes that recur in his journal and letters:

- 'Christ in me the hope of glory.'
- Spiritual warfare, and all that that included.
- The importance of being transparent.
- Praying and waiting on God for guidance.
- Seeing God guide them when a group prayed and waited on him.
- How to intercede for nations and cities.
- Learning more of God's ways.

He was reading Acts 11, about how the apostle Peter took the news of the Gentiles having been saved to the circumcised Jewish Christians. The Holy Spirit was opening up spiritual truths from his reading:

First disunity in the church; first fight over doctrine. 'The believers criticised him **[Peter]**.*'*

BUT [Peter explained saying] . . . 'who was I to think that I could oppose God?'

(LORD, I never want to oppose you, in what you are doing in others, or your process in me.)

After the brothers heard this, though, 'They had no further objections and praised God, saying "So then, God has granted even the Gentiles repentance unto life."'

1. A great example of how to react to differences. They praised God = humbleness, obviously. Also, recognising God as sovereign. It was nothing they did and not really their business. Do people fight for personal victory?

2. Quite a revelation to them about the Gentiles. Again no pride = us. 'Oh. I thought we were the holy people of God.' NO = God has granted + praise.

And a comment on Acts 14: '"Paul and Barnabas went as usual" (it's biblical to repeat evangelistic techniques).' He drew a smiley face, to emphasise the point.

It was also a time for setting his life's course

Crossroads today = saying be a radical. I desire that.

I am 18 years old. My life has been [he drew a wiggly graph]. I am scared, concerned that during the next year or so I will grow cold. I don't desire that. I desire to grow every year. I desire an intimate relationship which becomes stronger.

I question my motives. To get my photo on the front of Renewal [an English Christian magazine]? Somehow I know that's not it, because I desire to know God, that's all.

I want more than anything to have this. I admit one reason may be selfish, as I don't want a material, pointless life. I want to be radical, about the one thing which is worth being so about, therefore I'm a 'SLACIDAR' ☺ [When I came across this in Pete's journal I asked Dutch friends what it meant; they said it wasn't a Dutch word. Then I suddenly saw that it was back slang! (Try reading it backwards.) I think he used it at youth meetings too.]

I seriously, so want to be a radical though. 1st – God-knower, 2nd – God-server.

Man, at least God, I want to be 'a man after your own heart' and do everything you want me to do.

I must have a quiet time with God each day.

Another day, fearful that he would not be able to go on being a witness to the Lord, he wrote a cry to God:

Lord to know your heart, what you see in the church, to be able to serve you. God, NOT to get bored, no never, to learn some.

GOD HEAR ME, O GOD MOULD ME, I CRY. TAKE ME GOD, PLEASE, TO YOU, FATHER. WORK. BUILD . . . PLEASE.

Near the end of the course he made a special promise to God.

Floyd, speaking on pride this morning, challenged us to make a covenant with God to keep us from pride. I want to, and feel a peace, though I'm apprehensive about doing it. The wording won't be perfect, but God knows my desire.

Therefore, on Tuesday 26th November, 1991, 3.30 p.m.:

'God, the Father, Son and Holy Spirit, I choose to make this covenant with you. That you will lead me to an intimate relationship with yourself, break me to meekness and bring me to be available for any plans you have for me, by whatever means you choose to do so, for your glory and victory.'

I want to be open and transparent to my God.

He was still full of fun and kept his 'Kenyan' identity; wearing a *kikoi* for a scarf and another for night wear. On the Steiger fliers he was billed as 'Peter-the-Kenyan Jackson!' And one of his fellow students later wrote, 'Whenever I see my husband wear flip-flops with socks, it reminds me of Pete!'

He also, practically, learnt a great deal about God's guidance

Although he had originally wanted to go to one of the very distant outreaches, he later wrote to us:

I really felt it right to go to Budapest. We've got a great team of only six, though, with a fantastic leader, so I much look forward to that. −10° will be fun!

We are now into our second week of one month of Holland outreach = v. interesting. First two days we had open air services in central Amsterdam and a housing estate. Then one of the staff felt that he was directed to set up a ministry of having people on the streets 24 hours, 364 days. So he got us students to do one 24 hours, in shifts to see what God did through it.

I went out on the second morning and had a really amazing experience. I was with a Dutch guy and we both felt apprehensive about just walking up to people and 'witnessing'. So I said it out loud very plainly in a prayer as we walked into the red-light district. Five minutes later I saw a street guy I'd met before, he was hurrying off somewhere so unable to talk but, by 'coincidence', he was just talking to another guy who it was easy to go up and talk to. Within 3 mins of conversation, this guy brought up the subject of life after death . . . Wow = 45 mins talk.

Jonathan was in Amsterdam for business that night, so he stayed here. It was good to see my executive-suited brother zoom through town.

Now we wait for next week. Briefly, the leaders have felt that they should do something new with this school, i.e. they've split us into groups of four and given us ten days to go out into Holland and do whatever God-would-have-us-do! That's next week. We can't stay at De Poort. I'm with a great group, though after three hours of prayer we've no idea what we should do, so we can only wait and trust, but that sure is not easy.

So wrote the slightly Americanised boy! He later wrote how scared they felt. It really meant going out on a limb, and some felt it was too much.

I mean looking back on the ten days that we were out of the school there were so many details where I can see that the Lord personally directed us or provided. That reality of him is something which is being really, really fresh to me.

After praying for two evenings, we had a name of one town which we felt it right to go to, so we went and found accommodation. Literally the morning we left, some Dutch man gave me an address of a couple. So we went there and were welcomed by a very surprised couple. We had a very learning-full four days there, finding a small but rapidly growing church in a very dark, Catholic/occult-ridden town. It was amazing, as we just sat in the house, Christians just phoned to come and visit us. We prayed and talked with them = a v. good time.

Anyway, Tuesday evening, we thought we should pray about whether we should move on. So Wed. morning we had a prayer time. When we weren't sure what to do a girl said out of frustration, 'Well, I think we should go to Maastricht.' What?!! That town had been on my mind since I had woken. She said she'd seen [a vision of] it imprinted across her own forehead. A third person had also had it. So off we set to the other side of the country. To say briefly again.

The girl had written down a phone number of a pastor, from about 20 numbers in a book. So we phoned a rather wary pastor who gave us a number of a lady. On phoning her, this is what she said. 'Praise God you listen to him, I've been praying for people to come.'

So, we went. And looked after her house for 3 nights. It's all quite incredible and I really am amazingly thankful, again, that I've been able to do this course. I mean just this evening we went to a student bar and I got talking to a Muslim fanatic. It was a good time. Mum and Dad, I desire and pray so much that any fire/zeal I have now will be consistent and not get drowned as I go to university. I really think that is my major request for prayer. This place just speaks of what God is doing right across the globe, and man, I don't want to miss out in this plan!

He had been rather overwhelmed at first, finding himself with such a crowd of folk from different countries, including married couples and many people older than himself. (Some were even already on their way to full-time missionary work.)

But when he had his 19th birthday, he was surprised and warmed by being inundated with cards and good wishes from his class. But still he often felt rather lonely and different. Thinking of all of us in Kenya over Christmas, he prayed that Rozi, who also could not be with us, could visit him. 'And guess who phones in ten minutes?' he wrote in his journal, 'It seems a sister is coming.'

After all the excitement of the Christmas outreach and Rozi's visit, he felt his 'consciousness of God' had died down. But, he notes, 'God is still obviously about.'

He must have been concerned about the cold in Budapest.

I heard of ski jackets for 100frg in one shop, so prayed that if it was right to get one I'd find the shop, then a good jacket. After a 30-minute walk . . . I failed to find it, so back-tracked and walked into a clothes shop I saw. First thing I noticed were 100-guilder jackets. . . . After half an hour of deciding, I bought a very nice jacket. Guidance about a little thing.

That night I was feeling lonely before supper, as I didn't really fit in the pre-20 group. I prayed at supper. I jus' volunteered to do something, and Bonny-Jo stands up and says, 'I think Pete Jackson is a very nice guy.' God is so good.

He would have been very surprised to have known what the YWAM staff thought of him too. One staff worker wrote later:

Until I met Pete, I'd never met anyone his age who so obviously had told the Lord, and meant it, that he could ask anything of him that he wanted to and he'd be at peace with it. Everyone knew it; he'd never have said it, and he didn't have to. . . . My daughter says that she's never met anyone who had such peace. Who had a maturity that you usually see only in older people, who had an aura of God about him, who had obviously 'settled it' in himself.

25

Budapest

The great day came to set off across Europe. Pete was very pleased that his team leader was to be Jim Isom, whose lectures he had so much appreciated. He told us later that the journey was pretty awful, if interesting: seven of them squashed into an ancient, six-seater van with bad suspension. But it was Jim Isom who told us that 'Pete chose to sit in the middle of two seats. He made a pillow of a coat and never grumbled.' A photo of the group shows him with his usual cheerful grin.

Maybe he was more used to long journeys than the others.

We were glad to get his letter:

I'm in Budapest!
   We had a phenomenal drive here through West Germany, Czechoslovakia [I think he meant Czech Republic!], Austria, and then Hungary. Driving from West to East Germany was incredible, the road, housing and vegetation changed instantly. The towns literally take one back 20–30 years.

Budapest is interesting! Our hotel is an old fortress on top of a hill in the centre of the city, overlooking a park, the river and old Budapest. It has remarkable cathedrals, palaces and buildings, but all very old. But there has been quite a bit of western investment, so influence is notable. Anyway the hotel is different from De Poort. It is a complex of casino, topless bar and restaurant, the hotel itself being quite small and seedy, but our room, four beds and three in it, is relatively large, great view and heavy pounding of bar music from 11 to 2 or 3 in the morning. I'm sharing with an 18-year-old guy, v. nice, and our leader, who worked with Dave Wilkinson/Nicky Cruz for 10 years or so = Great. [The 'guy', Aaron, wrote later: 'I was Pete's roommate in Amsterdam and we were together on outreach. Pete was the best friend I've ever had . . . Your son would seek God daily and taught me the meaning of childlike faith . . . I miss him more than I can say.']

Our main work here will be with two great guys who started a house church here in the summer, the beginning of YWAM, Budapest . . . Prayer that we should be used to really strengthen this church I would really appreciate.

Anyway, anyway. I will try and write more regularly than before, I trust.

Muchos love,

Pete, one son J.

Three months later, as we sat round the dining-room table in the heat of Nairobi's 'summer', he showed us the pictures of the fortress-cum-hotel, still with many pockmarks of bullets on it, and the landscape of beautiful old houses that was their view. Beyond, were the drab tiers of flats that the Communists left behind there, as in the Czech Republic.

'We must remember we are not tourists!' Jim Isom had reminded them.

Pete wrote in his diary, 'The city is beautiful . . . I really want to be looking to God as to why he brought us and being available.' They had a little more free time than usual to begin with, so Pete used it to work on his Bible study of Acts.

Acts 16: Paul and Silas in Prison
I'm still learning of the reality of my God. I read in Numbers yesterday that God said to Moses 'as sure as I am real.' That made me think.

In this passage a girl, totally unconnected but possessed, cries, 'These men are servants of the Most High God, who are telling you the way to be saved.' That's awesome. I find myself thinking, 'Help! We've got 2.5 million to evangelise in this city, can they really be saved?' But the demon spoke the truth. What these men are said to be doing, is what we as a team will be/are doing, that is what I desire to do so much.

Thursday
Yesterday was great. We went to Jim and Gill's place and talked and prayed in the morning and evening. An encouraging introduction.

Driving back in the evening with Jim I and Sandi, Jim spoke a bit about his drug work. He said, 'All I have done and aimed to do, is to find out what God wants me to do in his plan and do it, leaving all the rest to him.'

That's basic, and yet the product of that is awesome = woodpecker and lightning effect. [He is referring to the story of a woodpecker who, seeing the destruction of 'his' tree by lightning said, 'Look what my pecking has done!']

This is so that God leads us to do the right thing, at the right place, at the right time.

I'm in Budapest because God wants me here. GOD wants me here. I don't want God to want me here, he actually does. So what does he want of me? To pray and seek a Most High God.

Acts 17

It is amazing. At Philippi, Paul and Silas get mobbed, attacked and then put in jail, God gets them out, so they realise they can't serve God effectively being so tired so sail out to a Greek island for a three-month sabbatical ... NOT! They walked 100 miles to Thessalonica, spoke on Sabbaths in 3 weeks, then got mobbed again (at least friends did) and they escaped by night.

On to Berea, and although the Bereans acted well, the Thessalonians followed and mobbed them again.

To me that all speaks of perseverance. Why was Paul so persevering?
1. His vision of God = he's real + big enough to be worth it.
2. These people need to know this.

In the following days he was encouraged when, after praying specifically for two people, he saw God answer that very day for the one on the team. For the second, he had God's peace that he had said what he could.

Sunday: Acts 18
Yes, I missed yesterday. I slept until we left to get to a baptism at a spa place, of three people. After a delayed lunch we prayed on a hill overlooking this city. I prayed that all the churches would become committed to the Word alone. We then watched a film, Fisher King = bad move. Bad attitude to God, street people, life, language, etc. Team dynamics come in as one of the group goes on about how good it is. I really want to talk to her about this stuff. Anyway . . .

[He notes how Paul tried to persuade the Jews but] They were obstinate so Paul moved to the Gentiles, where a church grew.

Here I am in Budapest. I represent God. I so want God to work through me. I believe I should pray that I should be prompted to step out if or where it is right to; to be ready to do anything the Lord wishes. I know I can be reluctant, I want not to be. Just to be really used, itakuwa mzuri [it will/would be good]!

Monday
Reading That Hideous Strength. C.S. Lewis makes me think more about the bigness and radicalness of a God. Gill really has a desire for God and that is what I want.

Acts 18:18–25: Priscilla, Aquila, Apollos
It's interesting. The night before coming to Budapest I went into De Poort Library and asked

God for the right book, having just spoken of C.S. Lewis's one. As I opened my eyes I saw That Hideous Strength. That shows me the awesomeness of a real God.

Coming here, Gill's hunger for God really impresses me, in Numbers I read God saying, 'as real as I am real'. What a quote!

Last night I put on Keith Green. The first thing that came out was the 'Bananas for Jesus' quote. [Keith Green was a Christian songwriter who died while still young. One of his songs was on the theme of 'going bananas for Jesus'.]

Anyway, today we meet Apollos. He was an Alexandrian Jew. He was a learned man. He had a thorough understanding of the Scriptures. He spoke of Jesus with great fervour, although only knowing of John the Baptist. The disciples took him and discipled him, and he 'vigorously' continued. Here's a man who didn't even know Jesus, but understanding the significance of God, sold himself for it. That is what I so desire.

I cannot say 'Right, sell out.' OK, I can accept God as a reality, but follow? Man! So I have to, again, ask that God will show me how to do this.

The next few days he went on to read about Paul in Ephesus, and the riot and obvious attack of Satan on Paul as he was opposing idol worship.

I in no way want to see Satan opposing us. On the other hand, I believe God led me to Budapest and I want to do what he wants me to do. This is likely sometime to include advancing God's kingdom + pushing back the other.

Friday: Paul's Farewell to Ephesus

Reading this passage, one statement leaps out:
'However, I consider my life worth nothing to me,
if only I may finish the race and complete the
task the Lord Jesus has given to me – the task
of testifying to the Gospel of God's grace.'

My response to this is one I don't feel all
over. I know it is correct, though, and I want to
want it with all of my heart, strength, soul and
spirit. This is sure: I want to do the task, but
not without a craving, seeking of God + his
love, in his peace + grace, without compromise.
So in this I seek his will in all that I do.

Satan was opposing him more than Pete realised. After
writing about him, the very next day, they were having
a time of prayer in a church. He writes: 'I still have
much to learn in just knowing God. Interestingly,
in prayer I asked for guidance on what to pray
for and felt a real anger at [one of the team]. I
don't know, but Sandi said she believed the
church needed to forgive, so I kind of agreed with
her from my feeling.'

He did not comment on this again except to say,
'That evening the service was very good. Jim spoke
on forgiveness.'

The next day, things were going much better. They
practised their drama (Pete had been cast as the leading
character), worked in a soup kitchen, did an outreach,
and 'got rid of a lot of tracts at last, and at two
commitment calls 8 hands went up. I pray that
Christ really grabs some of these people.'

He felt rather guilty that they were not more active,
but wrote: '[Paul] was left carelessly in prison for
TWO years. I mean, God allows this. What for I

don't know. But being here, I don't feel guilty for not doing anything, so long as I have my quiet times [he meant spending time by himself with God – reading the Bible and praying].'

After three weeks in Budapest he wrote to us about his time there:

It is very interesting being a short-term student missionary here. Amsterdam seems many many miles away (it is) but also many moons ago.

What have we been doing? It's actually very different to what I had expected, to an extent. Hearing that the summer DTS [Discipleship Training School] had 900 addresses of people who wanted to follow Christ, I expected to be spending 24 hours a day on the streets doing drama, etc., but we've only had 3 shifts of two hours in 3 weeks, though those have been good times. Due to a change of law, for the second and third outreaches we had to be outside, not in subways. We went out for the second time and found a place but after 2 hours hardly anybody had even noticed us. Two days later, out we went again, a bit earlier and a different location I suppose, but crowds stopped to watch. We prayed for a number of people so that was, wow!

Two great YWAM guys started a major work with this church in September. It meets in a house, with about 30 people presently attending it. We have gotten involved, and also have got to know these people, which has been very good. This short-term mission work is odd work, as it is hard to be sure what God is doing through us and how we are meant to be working through a day when we have only one thing scheduled. However there have been some sound conversations and times with the church people. I have got to know some younger guys who are recent Christians and in casual talk one trusts that they can and do learn. They seem to have really big problems with non-Christian parents.

Other things. There is a Mother Teresa soup kitchen for street people here. We have been going in pairs to help there two afternoons a week. That has been good, and meeting an Indian nun who is a lovely person and amazingly committed. I don't know if she's a Christian . . .

We spent all of last week in 4 schools, taking meetings and classes. It was fun, and some kids really took what we said seriously. Though, doing this 12-minute drama in 5 lessons in a row got tiring. In the city we travel everywhere by a huge public transport system of buses, trains, trams, metro . . . Well, trailing from school to school we had to take a big amplifier with us. I and another guy shared dragging it around.

So by the end of the week I was quite tired. This weekend we were meant to be 300 kms away from here at a gypsies' village, but last night our leader, Jim, didn't feel at peace about it, so we didn't go – which I must say I wasn't too upset about.

He is such a neat guy. (Look at all the American slang I'm using now!) Anyway, he's about 40, a smallish, wide, quiet chap, who was working with drug addicts in New York for 10 years, going on to be a pastor, setting up a 300-person drug rehabilitation place, then being led to Amsterdam for the last 2 years. I really feel that a major reason why the Lord brought me to this place was to learn a wee, wee bit from this man. He has a great, great sense of humour. We have been in hysterics all evening, this evening, as we are most of the time when together. He still cries with laughter every time he sees me in my kikoi for bed, or toga as these yanks call it. Anyway, his motto as such is 'just do what the Lord wants you to do in his plan, when he does.' Very basic, but how the Lord has used him. Boy, if I could learn that I would be v. thankful.

The rest of the team is fun. We have had some friction but not a lot, and are learning how to deal with this. . . .

On Monday we find out if we are 'in' Albania or not. I really trust we are. It sounds as though it will be one awesome time, as it's almost a '4th world' country if that exists. No cars, almost no food, heating, money and lacking some other commodities. Our leader feels it will be a time for prayer for the country which people believe God has a real plan for, but which there is still much apparent spiritual attack on. That will be another gruelling 2–3-day van ride on the equivalent to a semi-padded chapel pew, wedged behind the driver's seat of a van. Itakuwa **[it will be]** interesting.

I have to add, tomorrow night we're going to a ballet, then a Bach Magnificat on Tuesday as tickets for these are 150 forints, the equivalent of 40 ksh. So that will be good.

Knowing his mother's rare ability to leave things to the last minute, he adds,

I wonder how or at least what is going on at home right now. I mean is it vaguely, even questionably possible that by some fair chance the words, 'Shall we start packing' have fallen in the house? . . . I suppose I won't hear until March 1st, earliest, when I get back to De Poort. You have no address for me, sorry, I don't know how reliable this post is, but I'll put it on this letter.

Then he asks how plans were going for England and Kenya.

After the DTS it will be very good to see a Mum and Dad again, really it will. Though for how long that will be I don't know. Well, thanks for any letters that manage to barrage their way to me and much more, for prayer. Certainly a lot more has happened here and at Amsterdam than I've prayed for!

Mingi, mingi and much, much tonnes of love,

Pete Jackson
(This signature is on lots of tracts given to school kids. They come asking for it!)

Pete had made himself very popular with the school children. Again, he was teaching 'Our God is an Awesome God' as well as the plays, and a talk on comparative religion. One of the team wrote, 'There was a lot of laughter at the funny things he would do before class.'

Another team member wrote of this time, which with
its frustrations must have been stressful:

He was one of the brightest and most beautiful flowers
amongst us. He always seemed to bring a certain
cheerfulness to any gathering. His ruddy complexion,
compassionate eyes, and ever-present grin reflected an
undeniably joyful heart. Pete desired nothing more than
to follow his Lord.

Pete was a beloved friend. He was a servant of the
Most High God and to each person he met, Pete was an
intercessor. Pete had a passion for people. He listened
intently, cared deeply, felt people's pain, and longed
to see people freed from the bondage of sin. And Pete
laughed. He told great stories . . . we kept a list of his
sayings: 'That's not true!' . . . 'You're as predictable as a
fish' . . . 'Some peach nectar would be so nice just now'
. . . 'Hello Memsahib!'

My favourite memory of Pete is of him in his navy
down jacket and scarf, cheeks red from the cold. He'd
been out walking – praying. That's where he spent time
with God. Pete walked a lot and you can see in his eyes
that he'd been talking to God, expressing the pains and
needs of himself and others. And this I will carry on for
Pete.

Things became harder as it neared the time for going to
Albania. On the Wednesday, Pete wrote in his journal:

First, I write this not recording a story to tell.
I want to write it for my relationship. If God
wants me to use it for others to grow, fine, but
not my story.

Basically, we got our visas today. Jim picked up
the phone and just had a 'Mr Isom, Mr Isom'
on the other end to the Albanian Secretary of
State. Amazing!

We went to a school this morning, firstly. On the way, we missed a stop, had the metro doors shut on us, and some got upset. Halfway through our first lesson there was a bomb scare, so we missed all lessons in the school. Sandi got angry and shouted out, generally saying it was a bad day. I know Chaunda was ill.

Anyway, after outreach tonight (pretty good, I mean God used it I really trust), we were walking from bus 7 to 27 when suddenly a skinhead yelled at Aaron. He rushed at Aaron, pushed him violently, then hit him hard on the neck and hurled him out onto the road, as a bus was coming. At this, Chaunda and I leapt in front of the guy and simultaneously said, loudly, 'IN THE NAME OF JESUS. STOP!'

There was confusion. He stopped, looked at us, then continued shouting. At that, a lady, then a man came in and took over the situation. The man suddenly pulled out a card – 'a policeman'! At that, the kid tried to run, but the lady leapt after him and tackled him. She was also police. That was an arrest and a miracle.

Writing to us about this incident he, typically, did not mention the part he played. He just said that there was a great hatred for Arabs and that Aaron was wearing an Arab scarf.

A little later he wrote again:

Other than that . . . we had a very good morning on Friday at a school where one really felt we were not just entertaining them but that the Holy Spirit was working. So that was good.

It's still very good meeting and getting to
know the Hungarian Christians and others
here. I think, at least it seems, that a lot of the
reason for our coming here was to meet some of
these people and encourage/befriend them. I have
much appreciated all that.

So, Albania happens in two days. I'm hoping
they have a post system and plan to send a
postcard to everyone I know the address of.
However, a 1200 km drive one way on a park
bench (equivalent to) wedged into the back of a
van is daunting.

26

Albania

YWAM had given Pete and the team a paper from a missionary working in Albania. It explained that the Christian organisation, the Albanian Encouragement Project, bringing aid and other help after the country had been freed from communism, had suffered many difficulties in 1991. They had called many Christians for an emergency week of prayer and spiritual warfare for this country in December. Also, it said that any Christians who could come after the prayer week for the long- or short-term to help them or just pray in Tirana would be very welcome. This was how YWAM came to be sending in Jim Isom's team, and there was great joy that they had been allowed entry. It was quite a journey getting there. Pete wrote:

<u>11th February 1992 Albania</u>
As I am so far behind in my journal + it's packed in a box in Amsterdam (~2,600 kms away), I've pinched, after much persuasion, a sheet of paper from Mr Jim Isom's journal to write a bit about this place I'm in; a bit about my DTS.

We had planned ~2-3 weeks in Albania towards the end of our outreach. So, on 7th Feb. we drove out of the Citadella Hotel, Budapest, to start our journey. We stopped over Friday night at the Hungarian/Yugo. border, at a school. We did 'The Seeker' drama with some of their students, then had a very relaxing evening, walking to a Pizza place, yakking + watching one movie. Jimbo, Aaronus and I slept at a nice but costly hotel.

Sat. morning, after planning to leave at 7.30 a.m., we left at 12.00 after Isom felt we should check the brakes which were slipping a bit. We drove to the Yugo. border to enter, for my first time, into a country that was fighting. [He told us, as we sat round the dining-room table two months later in Nairobi, that they had no idea of how bad the fighting was at the time.]

We had no problems other than two military road blocks, Sandi having Jim's camera snatched off her and de-filmed at the border, and feeling threatened by a scud attack on Belgrave McDonald's, as we sat there!

That night we found a motel along the way to stay at, which had had an immediate reduction from $21 to $15 each per night. Aaron and I soon followed Jim to bed after receiving a serious glare from someone when we attempted to have a squathole [a toilet, almost certainly of the kind that are just a hole in the floor] race.

We continued to play a game of draughts in bed, in which Aaron took an early dominating lead. But I did fight hard to make sure it was a long game . . . That was a good evening. Jim asked me to organise a bit and pride flooded in, so losing the game of draughts helped that.

Next morning we rose and all had breakfast at the motel, then drove off in mist at about 7.30 a.m. The drive that day was awesome. We drove through a lot of mountains, many of which had snow on, and saw Yugo. hamlets which actually weren't too poor-looking. As we drove into some very romantic towns, houses looked a bit more worn. We drove into Macedonia, which we learnt afterwards had recently become a State (independent). A beautiful place. We passed by a large city/town sprawled out at the base of a mountain range. The roofs were almost entirely red-tiled, with very few high-rise buildings. That roof colour with the blue sky + mountains was very beautiful. As we travelled further into Macedonia, the buildings certainly became poorer. All highways were tolled, so entry on to them was controlled. It was amusing to drive almost 50 kms beside, or near to, a wide highway, us being on a parallel but small, two-lane road. After getting lost in a town, a series of directions from different people guided us to a petrol station, empty of diesel that we needed, but telling us we were near the Albanian border. They gave us final directions which we followed, pulling up at the Yugo., at least Macedonian border post.

He described his amazement at what happened next – he hadn't imagined what a post-Communist border would be like.

At the Macedonian border, a soldier checked our passports for visas. This took a lot of time, giving Will the opportunity to talk to a Dutch truck driver who had been waiting 4 days for an Albanian visa. He told us the road was bad. We'd already been told of kids running into the middle of the road. He told us they also jumped on the van to unscrew tail lights, etc. That prompted Aaron to whip off the lights, plugs and all. We also filled up with diesel from jerries we had, also borrowing a can from a truck driver.

Following this, we drove 200 metres or so to the Albanian border post – very, very different – to drive past 4 or 5 lorries and wait behind two cars to get to the border. The wait in the end was only an hour, speeded up by one of the police speaking English and claiming to be a Christian. I trust he was: he certainly helped us. The hour's wait gave us time to notice low, concrete bunkers on nearby hills looking out across the border, and other interesting items like a watchtower and barbed-wire fences, all very run down.

I walked up to one truck driver and greeted him. He was Bulgarian and did not recognise that I was speaking English. He asked if it was Hungarian, then German, possibly Dutch – then finally clicked: 'Ah! Anglaise, Anglaise.'

I was amused as a shaven Albanian soldier walked up, realising there was little Albanian/Bulgarian language communication, pointed to him and asked 'Visa, visa?' The driver said 'No' (i.e. shrug of shoulders).

The soldier's reply was 'Ah! Problem! Problem,' at which the driver replied, repeating that twice. Next, the soldier pointed at the tanker on the lorry questioningly. The driver said, 'Whisky, whisky.'

The soldier hesitated looked at the man and said 'Ya! (probable translation) Probleem. BIG probleem!'

Anyway, we were handed our passports after a search of the back, not very thorough, and set off, praying for safety and with locked doors. Four men in a car whom we had met at the border had actually waited for us, and led us halfway to Tirana, their fast driving kept Jimbo well entertained. The drive was a wow. Kids running out, pointing at their mouths, for gum. Two petrol stations, consisting of one tiny lottery-type office + an inconspicuous black pump. I saw probably about 5-7 factories: huge, solid constructions. Maybe one was workable, the rest, all in red brick, were totally derelict and empty. That amazed me. We came to one town, an hour before we expected to get to Tirana. On confirming with someone that it was actually a different town, and not Jim's speedy driving, we headed out on another road. As it was becoming dark, we stopped outside the town to replace the tail lights; this opportunity was exploited as a choo stop. We actually had problems with the tail lights, but by force insertion of bulbs and swapping some fuses, we had all but the brake lights working.

Another interesting sight after the military bunkers we saw at the border were small concrete dome bunkers everywhere in the countryside. This was just a part of Enver's un-understanding. [Enver Hoxha (1908–1985),

Communist leader of Albania for forty years. His regime was isolationist and rigorous, with extensive persecution of Christianity and other faiths. In 1967 he outlawed all religion making Albania the first authentically atheist state, an act described by his successor as 'a mistake'. Communism in Albania survived Hoxha by six years.] We learnt that there are about 3–4 million in the country. He had each family build their own with their own money, to protect themselves from the invading western armies.

Anyway, after our stop we continued our drive. It was about another hour on one narrow road, winding up, then down, through a range I think. Finally we saw a sign saying, 'Tirana 10 kms'. Expecting the typical lit-up sky, we weren't sure what to make of the sign when all we could see were some scattered electric lights. We eventually learnt that on account of a lot of electric appliances being imported, the electric system in Tirana was failing badly and there were regular power cuts in the city. So as we drove into the city it was almost in complete blackness.

They eventually found the Hotel Tirana, although there was no traffic control at all, and were able to telephone the couple who were to meet them. Pete went into the hotel with Jim to look for the phone. There turned out to be a room with three phones in and an operator's desk and an oldish Italian man with two fur-clad females and a range of Albanian men. They eventually got through and returned to the van to wait for their friends Grant and Sarah.

During this time, a clan of gypsies came to the van and – um – waited. I think Will first gave them an apple, as Chaunda and Kate cooed at the kids. Meanwhile, Grant and Sarah turned up and started talking. I got confused as the crowd of kids grew. I saw Will smiling at them with the door wide open, also noticed Katie taking off her jumper and handing it to someone, and hands reaching to a crack in Sandi's window, whilst every time a hand went up a tract, a big longish one, was handed out and grabbed . . .

Anyway, eventually Sarah got into the car and led us firstly to the girls' apartment, in an incredibly basic apartment block, then to the home 'us men' were to stay in, with a family.

Jim said that only Pete could communicate with 'the family' at all, and that was in his GCSE French. (So it had been useful after all!) Sometimes Jim would ask, 'What did they say, Pete?' and the doubtful reply would come: 'I'm not quite sure.'

In his diary Pete wrote:

We are spending two weeks here in the country. As communication to Albanians is not so hot, though we had a fax saying that Dave was happy for us to come, we had no idea of what to do here, other than pray for the place. We asked the YWAM and Albanian Encouragement Project (AEP) people if there was anything we could do for them.

The first day was generally just getting to know the place. Tuesday morning there was a meeting with all the AEP people and here we talked with one of their staff on what to do. She wanted us to go to schools to distribute Bibles, though it turned out that we were unable to do this, for although the government said everything was free, they still kept control over things like the schools.

They were, however, able to help in distributing clothes, shoes and Bibles and in unloading aid lorries. Pete wrote:

Very interesting work . . . I wonder how often in the future I will be doing that work . . .

We tend to spend 1–2 hours each day eating lunch at the Hotel Tirana. [Although lunch was more than a day's wage for an Albanian, it was very cheap for Westerners.] All cooking must be done on coal, judging from the black smoke pouring out from the top of the hotel, and meals are normally cold-to-lukewarm, particularly the fish and garlic spinach . . . UGH! They have a basic but good cake for pudding, the cream icing of which is good on the rye-type bread provided for the first course. That was Aaroni's discovery.

A postcard from Albania reads: 'It's a Saturday afternoon and we've driven far enough south to feel the sun – Hajabu! – as I sit in the park in the most non-running city I've known of. Anyway, you will hear more. 1 son Pete J'
In his diary he continues:

Anyway, often we have had, or it seems we have got, a free afternoon. Owing to the disorganisation and relative anarchy, we, or Jim, decided it's not such a hot idea doing street outreach, drama, etc. The wisdom of this decision was demonstrated last Tuesday, when Chaunda had the bag of tracts (it follows us to most places) and gave tracts to three men. Two more then asked for some . . . and in a matter of 30 seconds/1 minute, Chaunda, the very sweet girl that she is, had about 20 and growing numbers of men gathering and grabbing for tracts around her. Jim and I took the tracts from her, and Chaunda crawled out underneath.

So, Jim felt a very wise way of occupying time was walking along the streets praying in small groups. As we are foreigners, we always have people stop and want to talk to us, if only to practise English. What a wise way then, without having to force anything, to meet people and, if they are open, witness to them. Jim suggested also that we should tell them we are praying for the city and invite them to join in one prayer. We've done this a wee bit and it was good. It's resulted in us meeting a number of people and talking to them, either right there or in their homes. Talking with these people and those we find at the families' house has been good.

In his prayer diary he wrote:

I am still amazed at being here in Albania. It is a situation I have never been in, as many seem to be nowadays, and I trust and pray God teaches me, at least I learn (not the same thing) all he wants me to here.

I finished Acts in Budapest and decided to read a Psalm-a-day, more JI style, from Psalm 50–100 . . .

Psalm 62 some v. good verses:
My soul finds rest in God alone;
    My salvation comes from him.
He alone is my rock and my salvation:
    He is my fortress, I shall never be shaken
        (Psalm 62:1–2).

The first line makes me think. People don't feel at rest, only in God. Even as a Christian I know my soul often feels unrested. Only when I really look to God do I get this.

My soul = Pete Jackson: my actions, thoughts felt and needs. Boy do I think of wemales [women] a lot, and myself from others' perspectives.
Finds rest = rest boy = peace, with things to do, inadequacy.

Tuesday
I've spent the last two days, pretty well, in bed. Now sitting in the lounge-cum-dining-room in the family's house, I write a little of what I've been noticing/learning.

Being the eldest guy on the team, other than Jim, there have been a number of occasions where I have organised this or that. Man, and in this, pride flows everywhere. The first day, coming in, I remember being very prideful, and after that. Just the attitude, 'Oh, I've got leadership ability, I can deal with that,' really annoys. At least I know it is wrong.

Sandi, one of the older members of the team felt differently about Pete. She wrote of those weeks in Eastern Europe:

> Above all, I respected Pete's relationship with Jesus. His love for the Lord showed on his face when he talked about him or to him. He recognised the value of spending time with people and made a lot of effort to encourage the new believers he met in Hungary. One day in Budapest, Pete and I were having a hot drink and I remember him saying that 'God is just wow!' – he had no other word to describe what he was experiencing of the Lord at that point and I had such a strong sense of Jesus' complete joy in, and love for, Pete.
>
> He enriched my life as a friend. He looked after me several times, when I was in danger of being manhandled at street meetings. He was so courteous and concerned for my welfare in Albania and often waited to make sure the girls got home safely.

The time came to return to Amsterdam. The team packed up and started back on the exhausting journey across Europe. Arriving back in Amsterdam, Pete found it 'confusing but good' to meet all the other YWAM people again. He rejoiced in a heap of mail including an H. Duncan classic. (Harold Duncan was a missionary to the Esquimaux, was invalided back to England, became involved with camps and young people and, although at that time bedridden, had a great prayer life, praying daily for dozens of young men all over the world.)

The DTS were given a debriefing and time to share. Pete wrote down in his journal his reflections on what he had learned:

Confusing . . . very odd being back . . . In Budapest I learnt prayer on the battlements

was so good [I think he meant that Budapest with
all its communist links was like a fortified city as far
as Christianity was concerned. Being there he felt it
easier to pray for the few beleaguered Christians than
it would have been from another place. I imagine it is
a phrase from a YWAM lecture.]. BUT I feel there's
a lot more: NOT to get discouraged, etc., but to
look/seek for God.

Sitting down at last to write again, I say,
'God, please let me learn from your Word. I'm
not really going through much at the moment,
only thanking you for this morning . . .

Psalm 77: 'I cried out to God for help; I cried
out to God to hear me.'

I think straight to when I cried out to know
God. So much has happened since. I have much
to learn but he has answered my prayer. Even
in Budapest. Probably the most significant
verse of the DTS. I thank my God for that.

Thursday
Two things I want to write:
1. Dave was talking about 'Buffalo faith'. Using
   an illustration of animals and bad weather,
   he described how most animals in wind/rain
   stick their butts into the rain and back off.
   Buffaloes, however, do the opposite, and stick
   out their chin and face bang into the weather
   to 'Take it on!' Dave said, 'This faith, with
   God's strength, is what we need. Although
   the prospect of going to spend time at Orus
   is not 'Oh no, it's so hard', there are definite
   cautions. Will I get on with the Pokot/Davises?
   Am I enough of a seeker? Can I pray well?
   Can I witness, etc.? Man, I can't, but Christ

can; he says he can. What I need to do is get a right attitude in relation to expectations, but mainly take a Buffalo faith . . . Not to feel unsure, etc.

2. John gave us 1 hour to go over Philippians. One verse came out which made me think. The idea had come up before. Philippians 2:12b–13, 'Continue to work out your salvation with fear and trembling, for it is God who works in you to will and to act according to his good purpose.' Kind of, if I have fear and trembling, that allows God to work. Now as I leave DTS, I have nought but a God who is alive and as much of a teacher now as before. Man, to come and rest in his shadow with him working = a smack idea.

YWAM gave them all a good debriefing and some excellent leaflets to help them adjust. One was called 'How to Grow as a World Christian'. I think Pete knew that already.

Jim Isom wrote letters to all his team. To Pete he wrote:

I have really enjoyed getting to know you and to have you on my team. Pete, you have a real warmth with people that disarms and makes them immediately comfortable . . . God has a specific plan for your life that is tailor-made for you.

He had.

27

Return to Kenya:
March 1992

We collected Pete from Nairobi airport. He was taller, and I found it strange to see him in a black tee shirt, though it suited him. His face looked older, his nose more prominent. Perhaps we were looking at the face of a young man rather than the boy we had waved off in September.

It was a tremendous joy to see him again. Though we were hectically busy clearing the house after twenty years' residence and the refugee programme was still in progress all around us, during the first weeks after his return we sat together after supper for many evenings to hear all about YWAM.

He was a great help to me with the refugees' Bible studies and the food distribution, but for much of the time he and Julian were sorting and packing our books. Many were destined for various Bible colleges, others would be taken back to England. In between it all, Julian found time to take him out for an hour's driving practise each day – which was important, because when he went to East Pokot there would be no one else to drive the Land Rover and no way of getting anywhere except by foot.

For it was to East Pokot that it had been decided he should go, to help with a water project. He was delighted. He had offered AIM's volunteer programme three months' help after we left. Most of the young people helping out were there for an entire gap year and were teaching in church schools, but that was impractical for only a term.

Pete failed his first driving test but immediately put his name down again. Sadly, there was much 'giving of chai' (literally 'giving of tea' – but it really means 'giving a bribe') for driving tests in those days. A candidate would talk to the instructor for a while and then say casually, 'Would you like to have today's paper? I've finished with mine.' The instructor would accept the folded paper, because he knew there was 500/- note inside it – at that time, almost half a month's pay for a labourer. A Christian, however good a driver he was, could only get through by prayer.

We prayed. The next time he tried, there were rumours of a riot in town. Julian drove him out to the test centre via the ring road. He was the only private candidate to turn up. I think the examiner admired his courage. He only took him round a short circuit and gave him the coveted form. There was great rejoicing!

In spite of being so busy, there were some things that I remember specifically about him during that month. First, his praying in our prayer time each night. We still had a free time for prayer after a Bible reading and Pete had often, in the past, prayed with the others. In the first prayer time after his return I smiled as he began with a very American 'O Gawd' – the one Americanism he had picked up from his many friends in YWAM – and I opened my eyes. Pete was sitting upright on our old green sofa, eyes closed but facing upwards as he prayed, so obviously speaking to the Father, to someone he knew well.

I also noticed a new steel in his character. Some evenings, I was fed up with packing and thought Pete might like to play a favourite family game such as Boggle. When I suggested it, invariably Pete replied, 'Sorry Mum, I'm doing my one hour of Swahili now.' He was working hard at the book and learning the lists of words. But he did jump into my Mini with me one day and we went out to the shops to get him extra shorts and things he would need. He remarked, 'It's nice to go shopping with you again, Mum.' I felt honoured and saddened. Honoured, to be wanted; saddened, because of all the difficult times he'd had trying to buy his own things – perhaps because of our own accidental failure to send him enough cash to cover the things he really needed. That shopping trip was important enough to me to be recorded in my own notebook, and I am very glad we did it.

Pete was particular about his clothes. I did not care for black shirts (when we got back to England I realised they were the current 'in thing'), but they certainly showed up his red-brown hair and green eyes most extraordinarily well, but green and orange suited him well too.

He had an air of authority about him too, in spite of his gentleness. One day, as I was giving out a little cash to some of the refugees who had special needs, two young men were causing a nuisance and refusing to leave. Pete just talked quietly to them and walked them down the drive.

In his journal, he mentioned his concern about his thoughts on women ('wemales') and marriage and what his real heart desire was. He had been shaken, when he arrived in England, to hear that we had been robbed in our house in Nairobi.

Some things come out of this:
1. I love my mum and dad.
2. Am I going to have such an experience? Thinking of [some of the girls he had been working with]. I think again, am I prepared not to get married in order to serve God? It dawns on me what that really means!
3. There is so much hopelessness in the world. To have Christ as my whole hope and to be able to share this is my desire.

And now, back in Nairobi, these thoughts about what his aims and desires really were came out again.

Tuesday 17th March
'Give me an undivided heart, that I may fear your name' (Psalm 86:11b).

'Undivided heart' = no women   } Only
= no sleep   } after
= no distractions } GOD

Saturday 21st March
I didn't have to rise at 6.30 this morning. Rozi's Psalm 20:

'May he give you the desire of your heart . . .' (20:4).
'Some trust in chariots and some in horses, but we trust in the name of the Lord, our God' (20:7).

My desire. As I sit in bed, my mind wanders. I wonder how I'll keep up my reading by myself? I question what my desire is. I know in my head, and man, I think even in my stomach, that to be a 'man of God' = my desire. One who
- knows God 24 hours a day
- has one serious relationship
- is obedient, yes sir!
- does not doubt, whatever people say to me = faith
- has Christ working through me

(i.e. not having to pray about me all the time)

<u>Tuesday 24th March</u>
Sitting in the car this morning, noticed two Somali women walking past, and I thought 'women' . . . etc. as I often do. In fact very often. But yesterday I was thinking, I cannot spend my life thinking 'if only'. That's stupid. One thing hit me this morning. I can long for wemales all my life = never satisfied.
   BUT if I do + Jesus and God = alright!

He read and rejoiced in Psalm 100 the day he passed his driving test and then started a new page in his journal.

<u>Saturday 4th April. Starting Jeremiah</u>
Kuanza [to start with], reading a glorious book *Behind the Ranges* by Fraser of Lisuland. [A big bonus from sorting out our books was that he had found much 'gold'.]
Two points come out:
1. A quote from an unnamed theologian: 'What is Christian experience? What is

Christian experience, but the secret history of the affection of the soul for an ever-present Saviour.' That's truth!

2. A note written in a letter by John Fraser himself: 'It is all IF and WHEN (I can/will serve the Lord). I believe the devil is fond of those conjunctions . . . Since the things that lie in our immediate path have been ordered by God, who shall say that one kind of work is more important and sacred than another?'

Introduction (to Jeremiah)
Time of ministry = 40 years. 40 years of walking with God and being spoken to by our Lord, the Most Holy God, who is there.

'The word of the Lord came to me' (Jeremiah 1:4) . . . I really would value that gift. Knowing what to say. 'The word of the Lord.'

Monday Jeremiah 1:6–10 Jeremiah's call, then answer:
'"Ah! Sovereign Lord," I said [very smartly, as I knew myself so well, being so mature], "I do not know how to speak. I am only a child."'

God's reply = '"Do not say 'I am only a child.' You must go to everyone I send you to and say whatever I command you. Do not be afraid of them, for I am with you and will rescue you," declares the Lord.'

Sort of relevant after praying last night for Pokot:

1. that I will really grow in confidence that the Lord is with me.
2. that I will really see the Lord work through me.

I THINK THIS IS IMPORTANT FOR UNIVERSITY

During those last weeks, most evenings were spent visiting friends for supper (which Pete really enjoyed) or having guests ourselves. There were so many friends to whom we had to say goodbye.

One evening, our guest was an older woman whom Pete did not know and thought would be boring. He wrote in his diary afterwards:

Bonus! Pearl Laver came to supper tonight and she was a fire in Christ. I so easily judged/ condemned her. MAN, me-I've-got-it-sussed type attitude. I feel so fat with pride about me, my leadership possibilities, my maturity, my wisdom, especially on Christian matters = sucks. S.U.C.K.S.

I pray everyday for reality . . . for pride to go, even talk to Mum and Dad about it.

Sadly, I don't recall him ever doing so. It was hard not to be proud when the refugees were calling him 'the flower of the Jackson family' and he was the only one at home doing all the hard jobs for us.

We did talk a great deal about our memories of that house and what he had particularly enjoyed.

'Sundays were always nice, weren't they?'

'No, I really hated them.'

'Oh Pete! Why?' I said, aghast.

'It was having to wash up,' he replied with a slow smile.

We did laugh at that. We had always gone out of our way to make Sundays happy times, but because it was the only day James had off, we did have to wash up our own dishes. When he was very little, Pete was excused, but the others soon made sure he took his turn.

Long ago we had decided that in the week before our last Easter we would visit some of our good Kenyan friends who lived in Eldoret and Kitale, to say goodbye to them before we left. So we set off, taking it in turns to drive, and were especially glad to have a young, strong driver to help us. I somehow found time to write down thoughts during the journey. The Limo family in Eldoret were especially kind to Pete and asked him to come back and stay with them for longer in August, to which he was looking forward. We also went to say goodbye to that amazing woman, Patty Drakely. We found her sitting at her front door, where helpers had carried her; she was immobilised by a fall that had broken her hip. A doctor had told her it could not be mended. The pain must have been terrible, but she was delighted to see us. She asked us what we thought about the Bosnian situation: I felt stupid, as I knew nothing about it at all.

She talked about Jesus. She'd had a vision of him standing in her room. She could only see his feet and a bright light. She tried to move her eyes higher, but could not. He said, 'I am coming for you, very soon.' That was so comforting for her. We later heard that she slipped into his presence in July. What a triumphal entry it must have been.

Pete had been so glad to see her again, and was delighted to have his first chance of driving through mud, on the road to her house!

His mind was still very much on Pokot; he was more absent-minded than usual. He came shamefaced from the shower one day, having dropped our last piece of soap down the long drop. But he was not absent-minded when driving. He drove well, driving almost the whole way back on the last day.

We finished the week by staying a night with James, our old cook, not far from Lake Victoria. It was a densely populated area. Wherever we went, Pete was surrounded by children. He took with him some of his best toy cars and Tonka lorries, which gave great delight to James's little grandsons. He had already sold his Action Man toys. I was a little sad that he was giving everything away. What about his own children one day?

I am glad I did not try to stop him.

On our return, Pete wrote:

<u>Saturday 11th April</u>
I've come back from a very fine tour of Mum and Dad's old friends. There were times when I really felt able to pray, for Pokot and specific people. Going to Baluya land [the area near Lake Victoria] and seeing the huge population, eh, nimeshangaa [I was amazed, astonished]. I really thought of so many of them in witchcraft, drink and immorality = I don't get this. But I was encouraged by a good church network about [James's house].

Anyway, back to old Jeremiah again . . .
'Get yourself ready! Stand up and say to them whatever I command you.'
Lit. tighten you belt:
• fills up the fear/ugh
• makes one presentable, something to be reasoned with
• shows one is alert

<u>Sunday 12th Jeremiah 2:1–12</u>
Firstly. God's first command to Jeremiah: 'Go and proclaim in the hearing of Jerusalem.'

Boy, that needed courage and the fear of the Lord to do it!

Continue to pray about Emile's words, 'Don't be inhibited, "British", speak it out.'

Then verse 2 speaks of leading Israel through the desert.

I think of my life: home > plans from school > YWAM > home > Orus > etc., how it all falls into place. I look at that, realise and react.

He saw that God, in his wisdom, was leading him from one place to another. He saw how the Lord was hurt by the rejection of his people, 'the blunt hurt of rejection'. He added: 'I know I need to burn up to know him. All my heart!' The task ahead looked so immense, enormous.

On Palm Sunday, Julian was preaching at an Africa Inland Church service for the last time. Pete was asked to read the lesson from Joshua 1:1–9, *'Do not be terrified . . . do not be discouraged, for the LORD your God will be with you wherever you go.'*

Afterwards an elderly missionary talked to him. The missionary recalls, 'We fell into conversation and Pete listened carefully as I responded to his enquiry and told him of our work at Alliance [high school] and our prospects for the future. He, too, spoke of his assignment. Without exaggeration, I left him carrying the strong impression that I had been ministered to maturely and lovingly.'

Maundy Thursday, the day of Pete's departure, came at last. I was so busy packing boxes and trunks, I remember Julian calling me, 'Aren't you coming to say goodbye to your son? He's just leaving!'

I came to the front door, with its huge gash of red beside it which was the ugly new security door that we'd had put on after the recent theft. Pete was squeezing into an estate car with his pack. The car belonged to one of the young AIM pilots who was also going to Orus with his wife and two friends for a break over the Easter weekend.

Pete gave us big goodbye hugs. His eyes were sparkling with delight, to think he was actually off. Our home was looking very drab and was in a mess, and it must have been very boring for him packing and selling our things. I also had a feeling that it was too painful for him to see everything go. The house had been the only real home he had known for his 19 years.

He had said a big goodbye to James and his son Bakewell, and rather a hurried one to Cobble, his much-loved dog.

So although I was sad not to have him with us for Easter, I was very glad for him to go. I knew he would enjoy being with all those young people.

He had been busy packing for days. He had sewn himself a new sheet-bag, made an amazingly presentable pair of shorts out of some old jeans, and had created a very good bag, a well-disguised camera case in odd colours and well padded with foam. He had made it not only for Pokot but for later on, when he planned to travel round by bus, to prevent his camera from being stolen. Also, his backpack was carefully packed with medicines and all his important documents in small dust-proof pots and plastic bags. Wanting to travel light, he took the minimum of clothes and left others in

Nairobi for his later travels. He remembered to take a present for the young man – a community health nurse – with whom he was going to stay for the next few months.

Catherine, one of the other passengers, says they sang much of the way up – funny songs and serious ones.

STAGE 3

. . . and my deliverer . . .
I call to the LORD, who is worthy of praise,
and I am saved from my enemies.
Psalm 18:2–3

The shield had turned bright as silver, and on it, redder than blood or cherries, was the figure of the Lion. 'Doubtless,' said the Prince, 'this signifies that Aslan will be our good lord, whether he means us to live or die. And all's one, for that' . . .

'Friends,' said the Prince, 'when once a man is launched on such an adventure as this, he must bid farewell to hopes and fears, otherwise death or deliverance will both come too late to save his honour and his reason.'

C.S. Lewis, *The Silver Chair* (1953: Penguin edition 1965, pp. 164–65)

28

Orus at Last:
'Why am I Here?'

From the ends of the earth I call to you, I call as my heart grows faint; lead me to the rock that is higher than I.
(Psalm 61:2)

Pete's travel arrangements for the trip to Orus had been changed several times; his original plan to go with the Davises had fallen through because their vehicle was full, and now he was travelling with a car full of different missionaries. It made him a little unsettled: *'Am I really wanted?'* he wrote to a DTS friend later. *'I know very much what you mean by feeling scared of living with people you don't know. I felt like that with the missionaries here.'* 'But,' he added in his journal, *'it was fun.'*

From Nairobi they travelled west to the edge of the Rift Valley, then north along its edge. Descending slowly down the side of the escarpment near Naivasha Lake, they headed north-west to Nakuru in the centre of the Rift, then north between the rolling blue Tugen hills. All places full of memories. They stayed the night at Timemoi, where a TIMO team – young people, largely Americans – were getting practical missionary experience with the Tugen. Pete commented that they 'were great' and their leaders 'sound'.

> We left at 9 a.m. Sat. morning to get to Orus for lunch. A standard Orus drive did in fact get us there for lunch, which was smack. I was to share a room with Jeff at the beginning. Really I felt odd there again, continuing to realise very much that I wanted to impress . . . humility is so important, just to look to God. I had shied away from that as it's hard to do so without being motivated for one's own gain.

'On Easter morning,' **Pete wrote**, 'we woke early to climb the hill with Reuben; that was good.'

The 'hill' was Chowit. It rises steeply on the east of the valley in which is the Davises' bungalow, and is the last hill before the Turkana plain; Mlam Tich is on the south of it. They went up there to praise God as the sun rose over the distant blue Tugen hills, I am sure bringing back for Pete memories of Easter Day in Portugal.

Later, they gathered for the morning service under a tree, the congregation slowly walking in. 'About five people said they wanted to believe in Jesus, which was a wow!' **wrote Pete**, 'so there were plans to follow them up.' In the afternoon, some were preparing a goat roast and others were relaxing with books. As Pete went to look for a book, Art asked if he would like details of the work he was to do. Art wrote it down for him. Pete kept the list in his study Bible; I think to keep it safe from termites. It reads:

- Help John fix connection of pipe from windmill to water garden (next to windmill. Water threader is at Orus).

- Supply water (using water trailer if necessary) to Kadekoi Nursery school. (N.B. be sure to use 4-wheel drive when climbing slight hills and going through river beds.)
- Work on road (especially dig water drainage ditches).
- Fix padding on Land Rover.

Other tasks included moving a *rondavel* at Katengwa onto a cement pad. Certainly such activities were going to stretch this ex-schoolboy. The list ends:

- Help visitors.
- Participate in church services.
- Do any innovative or needed things that you see.
- Lead prayer time every week.
- Have short prayer time and Bible lesson with workmen daily.

Rather subdued, Pete went back to join the others. That night he and three others, including Jeff, slept on top of a container; these are often used as extra secure storerooms all over Kenya. 'We talked late and I was woken early, but it had been good,' he wrote.

On Monday morning the other visitors left to return to Nairobi. Art and his family stayed on. The plan was that they should spend the next few days showing Pete what to do and introducing him to the church there. However, Art decided that first day to take the party north into the Turkana valley (Orus lies on the border between the Pokot and Turkana grazing grounds) mainly because he and Reuben had a great commitment to the Southern Turkana, many of whom had no contact with Christianity. He especially wanted to visit one respected

Turkana elder called Kanyuman, who had made some profession of belief in Jesus on a previous visit and had invited them to start a church there. That meant Jeff could do more hunting, and a visitor, Miriam, could see more of the country.

Kanyuman was a wise man who was a strong advocate of friendship between the Pokot and Turkana. The Pokot elders were glad that he had put up a *boma*[8] for some of his wives in the area beyond the valley that fell away below Orus.

Pete wrote, 'After an early lunch we set off with Reuben and two Pokot but minus Mama Jeff. I sat in the Land Rover the full journey . . . We drove a long way to a newly deserted Turkana boma where we set up camp on a nearby donga.'

The large *boma* was completely empty. There were the sticks of several deserted huts and at least three groups of three blackened stones where the three wives Kanyuman had kept there did their cooking. He had other wives caring for other groups of animals in other areas. There were also the remains of two large *bomas* – one for cows, one for goats (he kept his camels elsewhere) and an interesting semicircle stone fence at the top end of the 'village'.

'Whatever was that for?' Pete asked Art.

'That was where Chief Kanyuman entertained his visitors, sitting on that wall. Last time we were here, we sat there and played some gospel tapes in Turkana to him. He listened well and said he would like to invite Jesus into his *boma*. "I want him to walk with me on all my safaris for the rest of my life," he said with great sincerity.'

Art and Reuben were very disappointed that they all seemed to have moved away.

After supper they took a 'game' drive. Pete really enjoying being on the roof with the other young people, this time, in the dark.

We were beginning to head back, when DANG! We ditched a [he drew a half rectangle] species of ditch. We dug forward and got stuck; we dug back and got stuck. Two hours later (11.30 p.m.) we decided Reuben would take Jeff and Miriam back (walking!) and get the two Pokot and stones. By this time we realised we had to jack up the Land Rover and fill in [the ditch].

Again, the hour I sat on the roof with Art I believe was really prepared for; we had a very smack little converse. So about 1.15 a.m. or so, I fell asleep on the roof of the Land Rover, but back at camp.

It was a little more experience of driving in that sort of terrain.

The next morning, they went searching a long way north for any people. Pete was on the roof again, with Jeff and Miriam. But sadly, though they saw game, they didn't see a single Turkana – only several empty *bomas*. It seemed they had all moved away.

After one more night at Orus, Art took Pete and his baggage to Kokwo Toto, eight kilometres from Orus where he was to stay with Zachayo, the Christian dispenser. For the rest of the day, Art introduced Pete to people living round Churo. Pete's verdict: 'It was safi sana [really good]!'

Coming back and having much on his mind Art forgot to drop Pete at his new home at Kokwo Toto (KT) and drove halfway back to Orus. Pete chose to walk back. He stood and watched the Land Rover move off, winding its way between the larger rocks. The cloud of dust disappeared as the vehicle rounded the corner. He turned and started resolutely down the track. He was on his own.

'Thank you, Father. You never leave me or forsake me.'

The track followed a dried-out stream bed down the hill. Pete marvelled at the beauty of the Butere range of hills on his left, covered in low shrubs and even a few bright flowers. To the right were layer upon layer of mountains, with the steep slopes of Paka in the distance towering above the others. As he came down, the valley widened; on his left was the newly dug dam, and in front of him rose 'Colin's Hill', Kokwo Toto itself.

He passed some small *dukas*. One Somali trader was still open. Pete waved a greeting to him but moved on quickly: the tropical night was descending. He scrambled through the dry river bed, past the tree on the right that was full of weaver birds' nests, and up the track beside it to where there were several breezeblock buildings. He was hurrying now, past the new windmill on the left, then along the track through the browned stalks of someone's attempt at growing maize, past the new nursery school building and several of the mud or breezeblock houses, then – 'Good, that must be the dispensary!'

He began to rack his brains to remember what he had been told about his host, Zachayo. He had heard he was a Tugen who had learnt some medical knowledge from the hospital to the west, high in the Marakwet mountains: a Christian, who had come to help the Pokot people. He remembered that Colin and Daudi spoke highly of him. They also had lived with him while working there two years before. There was no other dispensary for at least twelve kilometres – one of Pete's jobs would be to drive for emergency medical trips.

He moved on swiftly, watching out for snakes in the last of the daylight, and rounded the corner to Zachayo's bungalow.

Rather shyly, he called out *'Hodi'*, the greeting one always gives instead of knocking on someone's door. He was encouraged by Zachayo's cheerful answer, 'Karibu'.

Zachayo's breezeblock bungalow consisted of a living room with a bedroom behind, where they were both to sleep on metal hospital-type beds. Washing facilities were outside.

'The first evening,' Pete wrote, 'was spent in a game of memory with Musa and Zachayo.' Musa was one of the young church elders for Orus and Kokwo Toto. He and his wife had suffered persecution from their families because of their refusal to participate in the traditional Pokot religion. His father, a very rich and influential man, had put a curse on them that they wouldn't have any children. So they had separated from their father's *boma* and were living in one of the other buildings on that ridge. Musa had learned to read and had also learned some tailoring – and God had blessed them with two children.

Pete later got to know well two other families on that rise. Charles Lowei, married to Rebecca, was a secondary school leaver[9] who had been appointed project manager. They were a very hospitable couple. John Tios and his wife Christine were employed to work with maintenance and evangelism. All of them, like Reuben and his wife, were from around Churo. There were still very few Pokot who had become Christians around Orus and Kokwo Toto, just a few women, no men as yet.

Pete has left no record of how well or otherwise he slept that night, but he was up early next morning. Art, Mary Ellen and family were travelling back to Nairobi that day, and they had planned to spend the morning at Lake Baringo Club first. As supplies were needed from the little whitewashed town of Marigat, Art wanted Pete to accompany them with the Land Rover, as it would be his first opportunity to drive it!

To Marigat I drove. John and the Somali refugee came with us. The Land Rover is a weight! But besides the distance it was fun to drive! After filling with fuel at the club, we left Art and drove into Marigat. John enjoyed this buying chombos [vessels of some sort], mbao [wood] and a first lunch. Eventually we drove back to Kampi where I filled up with mafuta kabisa [*mafuta*, oil or petrol; *kabisa*, completely] and gave John 30/- for chakula ngini [bad Swahili! But means 'more food']. At Kampi, I was introduced to the club manager, then went in for a swim (free) and soda (18/-). It was a good time. Art gave me his last instructions and I said 'Kwaheri [goodbye]' to the Davises! After another short swim, I drove to Kampi, found John and then returned to KT [Kokwo Toto]. With the long safari, I was knackered by the time I got back and slept much of the evening.

Friday 24th April 92
The first day peke yake [on my own] woken at 5.45 a.m. by a radio. I eventually woke up, rose. After breakfast of Malindi fruit and Bournvita we walked to the windmill to look at it. We came back via the big tank, where I

helped the Somali family get water. On getting back, I taught Zacay [Zachayo] and Ibiahim to play 'Pass the Pigs'. They liked that. Zacay then had some kazi [work], so I took my book and Bible to the dam then mlima [hill] to read.

[From the hill, he wrote:] Having just climbed up rocks and dirt by a dry river bed, I'm presently looking over a green but grassless KT. It's hot and these stupid flies are annoying me, but it's also very beautiful.

So I continue in Jeremiah 3:16–24. Man, these flies pester!

He then comments on God's comparison of Israel to an unfaithful wife. 'You know,' he adds, 'this is how much he wants us to follow him. Wow.'

At that time he was reading *The Father Heart of God* by Floyd McClung. He comments:

Floyd aims that through it [the book] I will have a better knowledge of God's character towards me. OK. So the Holy Spirit teaches us this. Anyway, after chapter one, he gives examples of flaws in authority figures which hinder our understanding of God. So far it's made me think:

- Having often been by myself, it may explain why I have had and do have difficulty in knowing God's presence 100%. Possibly independence – ME?
- All have been so good to me and Mum and Dad's allowing and giving of all my year off finance is such a hot example. Floyd uses the example of a small flower in the Alps of the

Alps, made so that one person would delight in it.

- God's affection = HUGE. I found the Lord, HE found me after so much pursuing. He dotes on us, is overjoyed by our development and successes, hears, sees our difficulties.

But he adds that he didn't manage to pray very clearly, he was so hot and hungry. He did read a little of *Father Heart*.

'I was hot, iffy and tired, but thinking, *Sasa ni karibu ya supper* [now it's nearly supper time].'

On his first Sunday morning, he went to the church and tried to pray with the Christians there. Finding it hard to concentrate on the Swahili, he wrote his diary instead – in Swahili:

I got up later than usual this morning, because of it being Sunday. I used a metal bowl to wash in, then we drank tea because Zac had been able to buy a little milk. When it rains we will get more. After tea we sat outside the dispensary door and prayed for 1¼ hours until people gathered around us.

Church started about 10.36 a.m. and went on for ages. I went in and sat with all the people. After church, I came here and got ready to help Musa learn the guitar. Zac burnt the githeri [a **rather heavy bean and maize mixture**] so he started again. After we had lunch at last, Musa came again and we struggled rather, as my Swahili is not good enough.

The conversation with Musa later took a disturbing turn.

'Pete, have you heard that the Turkana are thinking of raids again? Many people are getting worried about it.'

Pete's response was typically laid back. 'Do you really think they might come?' he asked. 'Or is it just a common rumour? We will have to pray about it.'

He didn't sleep well that night. It was oppressively hot, as it always is in Kenya before rain, and Zac liked to keep the window shut because of mosquitoes. Musa's words were probably going through Pete's head too. Although he was woken up by the chickens about 5 a.m. even before the radio started at 5.40, he did not really get out of bed till 6.30. He had to wait because, as there was water in their tank, the old Somali had come to bathe at their house. 'So I had little opportunity to read the Bible. We prayed in the church for an hour with the others.'

He made a list of the work he had to do:

- Make a short-cut road down to the main road.
- Take a motorbike [presumably of the Davises] to Orus after morning tea and the service.
- Go to Orus. But I've been waiting ages for the wazee [a term of respect for elderly people] to change their clothes.
- Return here for food and then take Charles and John to help those doing the work on the short-cut, to see if they are working well.

The list was probably written while waiting for the *wazee*. It is unthinkable for a person to travel in their work clothes! 'In the evening I walked to the duka with Zac and we laughed a great deal.'

Later there was more disturbing news. Two of Charles's children came round to say the tea that Zac had drunk at Charles's house the previous day had been found to have been poisoned. In the mercy of God, too little poison had been used to do much harm, but it was unsettling for a now very weary Pete.

He went back to reading *Father Heart of God*. His big question was, 'Do I really react as deeply to sin as God does?' And he spent time in prayer. His prayer list was wide: those in Amsterdam, YWAM friends, his family, each of the evangelists in Pokot, folk from Tonbridge, his goddaughter.

On Tuesday morning, he and Zac were woken with a loud bang like a gun. Though it wasn't a gun it made them jumpy. Probably these alarms, the heat and the lack of sleep rattled Pete more than he would have admitted. He wrote, 'David [an American from the TIMO team] came today. I was expecting him to come with his wife and stay a night, but they didn't, so I was kind of sad.' Behind this brief note there seems to be a sense of real disappointment. Between bangs, heat and rumours, he was feeling vulnerable.

But God had been teaching him to look away from such things. Clearly, at that moment the loneliness of the situation had hit him, probably exacerbated by tiredness, continual *githeri*, and he was missing people of a similar background to himself; but he determined in his heart to turn away from this.

'It made me think, "Why am I here?" In Amsterdam I remember thinking, "If I go to Orus, I will have a lot of time to learn from God, as he's with me and can continue to teach me."'

In Floyd McClung's book he read about God being his dad, 'one with a broken heart because of the sin in the world'. His reading in Jeremiah also made him see that God is a caring God. He realised that God had given him faith over the poison incident, and he was beginning to see that God could use everything that we experience and read, together, to teach us.

He liked that.

Rising Insecurity: 'It Would Be Very Smart to See the Guys Really Look to Christ in this Situation'

Pete was younger than those around him, but after a while he found his place as the driver of the vehicle. The rain had come, making everything cooler – and he had the fun of driving the Land Rover in mud!

He was still reading Floyd McClung. His comments on one passage reveal some of the inner conflicts he was working on at the time:

People say that to worship without feeling is hypocritical. But Floyd's answer = 'We don't worship God because of how we feel but because of who he is. Do it because it is right.'
- That says much to me about worship, about faith, about listening. Lose the vagueness; just do it.
- He is also wise about my insecurity. It's there – admit it. He says there are often problems such as self-pity and self-centredness. I think I had already realised that. So praise God, think 'God thoughts', write down the insecurity, write down what God thinks – then trust God for the impossible. Endure.

In spite of the ongoing rumours of trouble brewing, Pete was beginning to really enjoy his tasks. He was working hard each day carrying cactus in the Land Rover to be planted all around the edge of the dam, and working on cutting channels off the track that led to the 'main' road, to carry off the water when they had big storms.

At the beginning of May he wrote:

One of Charles's kids ran over yesterday saying there were some wazungu at the dam. Eventually Zac and I ambled over to meet them. One was a colonial and the other two were expats, though one of these had been in Africa quite a bit. They invited me to supper, so I returned later for that. It was good and I spoke mainly with the African expat of travels and Tonbridge on the whole. However, towards the end of the meal he said, 'I must be honest but I'm rather prejudiced against mission stations.' Giving his reasons as being the stations themselves are often rather unpleasant due to over grazing, etc. and, I think more significantly, speaking about the Africans (traditional) who become 'missionised', saying it took away a lot of their values. It then rained so I couldn't continue, even though it was only a small shower.

Walking away an answer came to me. 'Yes, I agree . . . but . . .'

Pete had some sympathy with this opinion. Like his brother, he longed for people to come to Jesus as they were, without changing everything and becoming westernised. He also knew that people would become westernised through brushing with others, whether they were missionaries or not – the Pokot, after all, carried guns.

It is such a privilege to finally actually live with these people. I'm slowly coming to understand the differences in culture. It amazes me how Zac has been here for 6 years, giving out dawa [medicine] now and again, playing chequers, talking and talking and hunting.

I've really enjoyed some of the work as well. Driving the Land Rover round and trying to fix the dam and road. The terungi stop [tea break – *terungi* is tea without milk] on Friday for some reason was really rich; sitting under a thorn tree with the casual labour and John and Musa, as they all laughed and talked. Mazuri tu [just good]!

But he realised the ease with which one could easily get into a rut in one's Christian life, just with the daily struggles of living. He longed to see the church people more on fire for Jesus. He underlined Jeremiah 6:16 in his Bible: '*Stand at the crossroads and look . . . ask where the good way is, and walk in it, and you will find rest to your souls.*' Beside it he wrote, '3rd May: Kokwo Toto. It's what we've got to do.'

There were other struggles beyond the daily ones.

Yesterday afternoon walking to the 'centre', I met a serious-looking Musa saying, 'Waturkana wanataka kuja!' [the Turkana are coming]. As Orus is empty of people due to previous scares, Reuben had climbed behind the Orus hill with another, to pray and read his Bible. They saw 60 cows in two groups, these being Turkana cows led by Pokot with guns. The Turkana follow these people. So, I drove over with John, Charles and Musa and after trying to pack all the Davises' and Reuben's belongings as best we could, we brought Reuben and family back to KT.

In the past, the young *moran* (Pokot warriors) would never have gone to war or gone 'collecting' cows without the blessing of the elders. But with the breakdown of some traditions, things had changed. The elders were aghast at what the consequences could be if the Turkana retaliated.

Pete wrote to us in Portugal, where we had gone for a week to visit Colin.

Here I am, back to the standard, following my brother but oh boy, I do not regret it, ata kidogo [in the slightest]. I'm writing this by paraffin light with Zachayo mumbling threats away beside me in a draughts game he is playing with another. Ni safi, bwana [it's excellent, mister]. Everybody is well, though Musa's eldest son has a stomach growth or something. AND there are Turkana problems . . . Every boma has been packing onto donkeys today, and they led them off to Churo/Tangulbei. There is no one at Orus and v. few here. We moved Reuben and family to KT this evening. Sooo everyone's kinda apprehensive. Just another experience for Mr P. Jackson.

But it has been so good, though only two weeks so far. They've put a smallish dirt dam in by the road above KT so it's been a lot of fun driving the Land Rover around getting cacti with the *vibarua* [casual labour] to plant on it, with John striding round organising. Musa's wanting me to teach him the guitar so I may try . . . there are now three shops here all run by the same Somali family, who are a great group, and three little grass *hotelis* [teashops] where chai is 2.50/- (about 5p). I find myself there most afternoons with Zac, John or Musa laughing at me drinking chai, etc. *Iko mzuri* [it's good].

But really people are taking the Turkana business v. seriously, understandably, as Zachayo, who always seems to know all the news, says most of the raiding *moran* came to the *hotelis* today for chai, one by one, which will lead the Turkana here too. Apparently Tangulbei is *jaa* [full up] with GSU [special police unit] and Turkana, but they can't get here as the road is a bath at the moment, even if we did cut, graze, sprain our hands, knees, feet and backs, etc., digging countless ditches last week [to drain the water off]. It would be really smack to see the guys look to Christ in this situation.

I trust someone is coming this week to take the post.

We prayed.

Pete wrote in his journal, 'KT is empty! Zac climbed Kokwo Toto yesterday and saw donkeys everywhere loaded up to be taken off [with fleeing Pokot families]. Only the ill, home guard and church people are here now, as well as a few *moran* and the Somalis.'

Reuben told me later that even the church people wanted to go. 'But Pete said, "Let's trust God

and pray and see him act for us."' Pete's journal
continues:

> We've all discussed what to do if we hear guns;
> there's a space made under my bed.
> It's amazing, it's all totally separate from
> the government, etc. [He meant the government and
> army were not involved] . . . but guns are still
> nothing much more than 303s. I'm actually
> in the middle of quite a realistic state of tribal
> warfare. Though exciting on the one hand, at
> one moment last night when I thought I heard
> a gun, exciting it was not. Charles, Reuben
> and John are hiding their cattle in the mstuni
> [bush].
> I've just heard a story that 40 moran went to
> this one mzee's [old man, elder] boma, killed him
> then took the cows and ran.

Later, much later, Art Davis told us it was the wise
Kanyuman himself, who the Pokot *moran* had killed,
causing great bitterness amongst the Turkana, and that
they had stolen 600 cows. Reuben was very sick at heart
about this. He and Art had so longed to plant a church
in south Turkana, and he'd had such respect for Chief
Kanyuman, who had asked them to plant a church and
with whom they had prayed. He was also troubled, as
were many wise Pokot elders, about the movements of
the young men – the *moran*.

Art and Mary Ellen were, reluctantly, back in Nairobi
by now and very busy with their other work of caring
for missionaries. They listened carefully to all the
reports. They knew Reuben was very wise and would
be alert for any danger. Also, with their experience
of the last raids, ten years before, they believed the

Turkana were only interested in cows and anyone who confronted them. They had never been known to attack any missionaries or church people. However, Art and Mary Ellen planned to go up to assess the situation in a few weeks' time.

Charles, the project manager, later told us, 'Pete was our friend, he was happy all the time and a friend to everybody. He told us, "Don't go and hide; God will look after us." So we returned to our houses and he helped us *kabisa* [completely, absolutely] with God's word. He was so keen to go to visit the people of Morogo who were saved at the Easter service, to encourage them.'

Pete cheerfully wrote on:

<u>Wednesday 6th May</u>
It really is empty here now. We heard yesterday that the Turkana chief told the police that the raiders are coming. I'm meant to be taking all the wives to Churo tomorrow. On top of this, I had malaria yesterday and I'm recovering from it and a Fansidar [malaria medicine] shot today. But that did not prevent me from going to Orus yesterday with John to make sure everything was all right, then spending 2 hours on the hill behind with Bible and 'Father Heart'. I finished the book and had a good time thinking and praying over some things I am feeling and thinking . . . I would not say I feel very 'spiritual' at the moment but as Floyd said, I don't have to do things governed by my feelings but by what is the truth. God does the work and I do what I believe I should.

His worry was not so much the Turkana as the prospect of working with older people again: the old tensions from his family that he thought he had laid to rest at Amsterdam; the fear of saying the wrong thing.

Me

I think a lot of this has come up with thinking about what's going to happen at university, when there will be a whole range of people, many of whom are not people I would standardly make friends with. The thought of being with 100% English is odd. Anyway, Floyd saying that the insecurity is from self-centredness is so true. With new people, I find a number of things. I am not relaxed, I feel an uneasy tightness. It means a number of things. It gives me an astoundingly bad sense of humour, when I say really stupid things. I also cannot be sincere and it is very difficult to make quality conversation. It's easiest to sit in an uneasy silence, which I really hate.

Though it would be true to say females give me the worst time, I find I have to live up to a 'type' - my Pete-Jackson sense of humour; also to be cool, relaxed and mature. Butt! It's the walking-on-a-greasy-ball syndrome when one can sort of feel it but then it's artificial, then it falls. The main point is, this happens because Pete Jackson wants to show these people who Pete Jackson is. They've got to think well of me = self-centred and self-orientated = a butt hole of a process.

<u>God</u>

On the other hand, this one's my Dad. He wants to be able to be proud of me, not out of a wrong sense, but wants to be pleased with his creation and delight in it being me, from my point. Christ has given me a gift of enjoying being with and talking to people. He is my Father. If I make (i.e. choose to make) him my centre I will not be trying to impress people by myself, which is an impossible thing to do, but am needing to be a witness, representative of God's impressiveness and what he's created me to be. Like that, Christ works through me, and O boy I have seen what that leads to. Right, they're not perfect, neither models, but Bentley, Brian, Floyd, Sandi, Rosemary, Auntie Patty, etc. are people mature enough for God to impress others with.

I need to have it in my mind that I am not impressing people, but I have a God, a Father who's working through me to show what he's created.

So that's something to pray about. . . . Only to seek righteousness and my relationship and God, and for people to be saved, the Pokot church.

The next day he drove the Land Rover the thirty or so kilometres to Churo with the wives and children. None of the missionaries were able to see him at this time; the road was almost impassable and he was disappointed that he was getting no post up from Marigat. He wrote to us saying, 'I wonder how Applewood is and how my parents are finding UK?' Not that he envied us. He wrote, 'I'm really enjoying staying with

Zachayo, he's a very nice guy. Asante SANA for letting me come.'

Reading Jeremiah and Andrew Murray's classic book *Humility*, his main reflection was the need to remain humble. It was difficult when he was 'the driver'.

An example was his competence at carpentry. Besides being awarded that grade A for the models he made for his GCSE woodwork examination, he had fitted up cupboards in his sister's flat, and of course he had far more training in these skills than the others at Kokwo Toto. But even this, he saw as a snare. 'Today's work [still Friday] has petered out, because I have a thumb blister, Reuben is looking for milk and Charles is still in Tangulbei. Pride comes up again today, in me being able to fix a door. In fact I made a stump of it.'

The Kenyans saw in him something different. Several of them said later, 'He was the most humble person.' They called him *Narakin* (the smiling one). 'He was always happy,' explained Esther. 'Even if he didn't understand, everyone wanted to talk to him because they saw he loved them and Jesus.'

Pete realised that it was vital to have his time with God each day. He would creep away to find time for himself up the hill with his Bible, Murray's *Humility*, the pestering flies and, of course, his red journal. 'To keep a daily quiet time really is work, but is so important,' he wrote.

Prompted by Jeremiah's cry that the Israelites were blind, he wrote, probably with university in mind:

The fact is that people are blind and go after the most pathetic things. I really pray that when people attack, I see their wrongness so much and answer in truth. Jeremiah sees how the nations who do not acknowledge God deserve only wrath.

I sit here thinking of the huge ecological disasters, political upheavals and social wounds, yet people still reject Christ. I suppose God only keeps us ticking for the Church . . .

Tuesday 12th May

Starting Murray's Humility today. It seems a smack book.

'Humility = the place of entire dependence on God.' The lack of humility is the sufficient explanation of every defeat and failure.

Wednesday 13th

What I write is the truth. Chapter 11:1-17 is God stating that because they have broken the covenant, so God's reply can only be the consequences. God is the Father, and speaks of the evils of his people, but still calls them his 'beloved'.

After hand-choosing these people and leading and training them into a beautiful prize country, he says all they had to do is obey him and he would be their God. Yet . . . they rejected him. God then sent his Son whom people killed, again in rejection. I can see God's heart must be broken.

Even in myself, I find it so easy to be complacent. The only thing Christ deserves is a heart given to God completely, as Murray wrote. I actually really did begin to seek that in Amsterdam, only to continue and learn. I find:

- Distractions come, like food and Louis L'Amour [an author whose books he was enjoying; he had found them in the Davises' house].
- Pride comes that, at 19, I'm so spiritual (butt).
- My motivations can be so easily for personal ambition: that people will say Pete, he's such a Christian or that I may become important. I know the irony. But the only motivation is that I owe everything to God, every slip I make brings grief. To humble this guy.

As in the story of Eve at the fall, pride is also Satanic in origin. [He quotes from Murray] 'If this is to lead us to utter despair, it will lead us all the sooner to that supernatural power in which alone our deliverance is to be found the redemption of the Lamb of God.'

On Saturday 16th, just before leaving for Amaya for a day of prayer, he read, *'For the eyes of the LORD range throughout the earth to strengthen those whose hearts are fully committed to him'* (2 Chronicles 16:9). He needed that!

30

The Long Sunday, 17th May: Work Resumes

'Kumbe [a Swahili exclamation]! The day of prayer at Amaya was very good,' wrote Pete.

The meeting had been convened for all the Africa Inland Church pastors and missionaries in the East Pokot area. From Orus to Amaya (where Art's brother Ray and Ray's wife Jill worked) it was a 56-kilometre journey that would take an hour and a half by Land Rover. Pete drove. 'However many times I stopped to let people out, it seemed the matatu-seating-style-squash was never eased; if anything, it only got tighter.' Driving off the 'main' road at Churo and the 20 kilometres drive into Amaya was really bad after the recent rain.

It was a real matatu ride . . . which I much enjoyed. The prayer time was good, having a list which the wazee prayed through in sections; probably about 4-5 hours actual prayer, so = very worthwhile. The chai, goat and ugali [thick, mashed potato type of dish made from boiled maize meal] were good too. [He had been living on *githeri* for so long.]

On arriving in Tangulbei in the morning, we heard a report had come from Turkana that, apparently, about 400 ngoroko [raiders] were coming to Pokot and were expected that morning.

There wasn't time to do or say much about it at the prayer time, and not until we [Reuben, Charles, Francis, John and Pete] met Tangulbei herds walking in the dark to Churo, on our way back, did I realise people were taking it seriously. And that they were.

We stopped at Tangulbei for a report from Richard [a Christian helping there with adult literacy], though we all agreed we had to return to KT, as Zac had stayed behind there. [Rather an ordeal for a weary, one-month-old driver.]

We set off with my one headlamp and realised that it had rained heavily at the top end of our road. I tell you, I'm going to remember that evening, because there were important decisions to be made and I did want to do what the Lord wanted. The first mud hole on the road truly was a mud hole + water – herds were still being moved away even at that time (probably about 9 p.m.). The water was still flowing and made the road a nightmare. We decided that rather than risk getting badly stuck in a hole, the rest of them could walk round it. So, by myself, as much as one can be after praying for angels to push at each corner of the car, I drove. I slid everywhere, but made it. Alleluia!

Zac had not heard the news at all, he took it pretty seriously.

Having just read about a Chronicles king being helped when relying totally on God, and due to the fact we did get through the mud, I was disappointed when Reuben said we should all go back to Tangulbei and sleep on top of a hill there. But as they were the wazee, I thought it best to go back with them. Charles took his car too this time.

We actually had a very rich time in Tangulbei. Stopping there, we were met by the spear-armed Hussein (the younger one) and the Tangulbei Somali, who invited us to their place for coffee.

They are an amazing family, those Somalis. A typical African trading family who have moved here. Sitting on the ground with them in the moonlight, drinking kahawa [coffee], waiting for the goat and rice they gave us, with the occasional wandering and wondering Pokot man with spear coming in was safi [excellent/ cool].

After probably two hours, we refused an offer to sleep there and took the cars up the hill above Tangulbei. We drove about thirty metres off the road and turned the cars, so they were pointing to the road. I left the key in the ignition and placed my glasses down carefully. Then both Charles and I sat in the driving seat to sleep, to be ready. It was interesting.

I couldn't believe it. John, Zac and Francis ALL sat on the middle seat of the Land Rover – refusing to come forward and sit with me – with sheets, blankets and feet and legs in all directions, saying they would sleep there. Every time I woke up, Zac was wide awake and sitting, whilst John and Francis still had legs dangling over my chair with their blankets round their throats.

Sleeping on the front seat wasn't easy . . . I frequently woke to turn round or to move a foot that was in my face; and when I woke. about 6.15 a.m., Zac and Francis were both up.

Eventually, we drove into Tangulbei to find only chapatis and men, but they had not been disturbed either.

Later, back at Kokwo Toto, a home guard came to the dispensary wanting John or Zac to mend his gun. It had jammed. He and 20 Pokot had met the Turkana, apparently only 100, and dissuaded them from coming. On Monday, we heard they had raided Kinyang instead, about 60 kilometres away.

Having read 'The Nation' [a Kenyan national newspaper] yesterday and hearing London World News too, I heard about the World Bank development plan and humanitarian plans, etc. I thought, these people are trying to solve world problems by being people. What I have to see now before I get to university is that sin problems are not solved by sinners. If the root isn't sorted out, what's above is a wild confused mess of compromises, etc.

Jeremiah had the same thing. Wondering why all the other prophets prophesied 'peace, peace'. The Lord replies, 'Those same prophets will perish from sword and famine.' I've got to hold onto these truths.

Coming over to Orus this morning to finish planting the cacti and trees that had been cut, I'm now really enjoying sitting in the house with stima [electricity (from the solar panels)]. We (Reuben, Zachariah and Musa na mimi [I]) finished the tree planting relatively early and, after a chai break, sat on the veranda and read 1 Corinthians chapter 15 together. My initial feelings were that that was not the time to read that book, but boy, the passage was good. I think the first two verses were the best, though the rest was impressive as well.

Verses 9–10: 'For I am the least of the apostles . . . But by the grace of God I am what I am.'

I have thought that I realise quite a lot for my age, though I recognise this is (if so) due to my parents and their prayers. That is not to say that pride is not in there deep down. It is – that's the truth. However, I have felt it's an injustice that I have that and others don't.

He thought of the 4.5 billion people who have not had the privilege of being brought up in a Christian home. He remembered weeping once in church, when he was 14, realising the huge undeserved privilege of it. 'It really was a Holy Spirit teaching this morning, not a mind thing.'

<u>Friday 22nd May</u>
All the men were at the dispensary for chakula [food] last night. They sat outside for space. As a group they will always get into some definite conversation. I think last night it was on politics and Turkana. As they talked on in Pokot, I climbed up on the tank and although at times I felt mighty frustrated that I couldn't join in, thought I might as well talk to the Greater. It was good. Earlier I had been feeling, 'Oh these

flies, these mosquitoes, these snakes (we killed another yesterday in the shower), this dust, heat, hardness, etc, etc. Whine!' So the talking was good.

This morning was Jeremiah 15. I said I wanted Holy Spirit questions from it. I think I got one. Verse 1 starts, 'Then the Lord said to me'. Who was Jeremiah that the Lord spoke through him? I would love the Lord to speak through me. Yes sir, to people and groups. To know what the Lord wants to tell them and to do it so humbly so that it is the Lord, and that the Holy Spirit can work. Mmmm.

He was thinking seriously ahead to university and how he would cope.

The next three weeks were a time for learning more of God. The rumours died down and people came back and work restarted. Pete found time to write many letters. Karl, Pete's school friend, once wrote that after receiving a card from Pete, he imagined Pete writing it, 'with his face six inches over the table and his tongue worming about beneath his nose; his right hand glued over two of the four corners of the postcard and his left hand scribbling down his thoughts.'

He still had not received any post.

He wrote of how much the DTS in Amsterdam had meant to him. 'It really was an amazing (awesome) six months,' he wrote to Jim Isom. 'Probably the most worthwhile I've had for at least the past 19 years. Learning that there really is a sovereign, loving God . . . Our 6,000 kms was an important part in that.'

He wrote that the difficulties had also been a time of learning for the church, though to YWAM friends who

were still working in Amsterdam he wrote, 'Although
the church elders are strong Christians, the church
is really dead and the people who become Christians
not totally changed . . . I would so like to see the
church here grow.'

The elders told me that he often took the daily
service, but he never mentions it in his journal, and
we have only one set of notes of a talk given at this
time. They are rather untidy and illegible as they got
splashed with water. He had spoken on Isaiah 53:6, *'We
all, like sheep, have gone astray, each of us has turned to
his own way; and the LORD has laid on him the iniquity
of us all.'* He spoke of the big and easy road that the
world around us follows. 'So, like sheep we choose the
wrong road. If I try going by myself I could be bitten
by snakes or attacked by lions or the Turkana.' But the
Swahili is so limited it is no wonder that Esther said
that he was hard to understand, but that they loved
hearing him because of his love for them.

<u>Sunday 24th May</u>
I was not going to wake up, but after John
slammed, banged the rondavel door loudly,
greeted me, then shone a torch, straight into
my face, I was awake enough to think of
staying in bed, but finally decided not to be
a slug. I struggled out of my *gunia* [sleeping-
bag] in shorts and slaps [I presume he meant flip
flops or rubber thongs that he wore everywhere], and
wrapped in a sheet I ran – stumbled – up the
hill, followed by John, to see the sunrise.

Jeremiah is good today. 'This is what the Lord
says: "Cursed is the one who trusts in man
. . . Blessed is the man who trusts in the Lord,
whose confidence is in him. (P.J.) He will be

like a tree planted by the water . . . It has no worries in a year of drought, and never fails to bear fruit"' (17:5–8).

'I the Lord search the heart and examine the mind, to reward a man according to his conduct' (17:10). These are pretty smart verses. I hadn't noticed the confidence in him before. I probably still have work to do there.

I love the way the Father says he searches our hearts – what blackness.

(By paraffin lamp light. I have to write or I'll go back to reading the next Louis L'Amour which I have picked up, which is only really fine in small doses.)

We went to church at Kadakoi this morning, that being six or seven branch benches round a shady tree. I don't think the two photos will come out, I'll see. It was an awesome drive there, along the pretty bad road round the base of Paka. We saw a beautiful herd of Impala, about fifteen I'd say, under shade. I'd say Impala must be some of the most graceful animals. But boy, just after the junction [of one dirt track meeting another] the grass disappeared. These cows are bad, bad. Sinakubali ata [I don't agree with it – the heavy grazing – at all]!

After a hearty supper of ugali, goat and terungi, Charles and Reuben have gone to sit by the fire outside with some visitors, two of which tried to follow in the return raid of the Pokot. I've heard of numbers between 300 and 500 ngoroko who've gone to Turkana for revenge. We heard this morning that 25 people have been killed at Baragoi and we presume, with these numbers of Pokot out there, they must be involved. We'll see what happens, possibly even move the cows if we go to Orus.

To us he wrote, 'The Pokot warriors returned exhausted, having found nothing but 9 camels!' Pete was having his turn of sleeping at Orus when they arrived.

I have never seen people so angry and tired, and all we had was tea leaves and salt. They drank it. Pole sana [I felt very sorry for them].

Anyway, after supper I lay, not for long, on the tank again and thought a bit. Louis's book on the taking of America makes one think. People trying and achieving so much. Then looking at the stars is awesome. If behind all this is a God who is what he says – Kumbe! Further, if I can have a personal relationship, that's a wow. If I ask him to humble me so I am nothing and he is all – not that I claim to fully, understand that – it's still nought but awesome. If he does, and by doing so, I become a channel for God to work through in a hurting by-so-much world, what could be better.

Tuesday 26th May

Flies again, feeling hot and tired, and now we have milk, there's no sugar. I started thinking what I hate thinking again. Prayed a bit, cooled down under the shower and drank some water, and I feel a bit better. As my clothes soak (3rd clothes wash in 5 weeks!), I want to write about the last two chapters of Murray.

But, I'm really writing this as though someone else is going to read it. Lord, that's so dumb of me. What I'm trying to say is Murray sees your grace in forgiving our sin, my unbelief, my pride, my obstinacy. You forgive and you gave me that family. Why can't I forget about being an almighty Christian? Only to be right, God, in your eyes, please. I need and want to understand your grace. Sorry for being dumb. Please teach me God, my God, my Father, my Friend and Companion, Lord please.

The next chapter 'Humility and Faith' is so, so true. Murray says we see the higher gifts of perfect joy, peace, fruitfulness, etc. but cannot reach them. Many are like that, as though there is a thick glass pane between. He says, 'What is the hindrance?' and says only 'Nothing but pride.' That's true. 'faith and humility are at root one.'

Wednesday 27th May

I sat in the Land Rover last night and told God I was/am realising how helpless I am without him working in me; that I cannot humble myself. I very much wonder if my problems in faith come from pride.

Jeremiah 18 had a very good verse today: '"O house of Israel, can I not do with you as the potter does?" declares the Lord. "Like clay in the hand of the potter, so are you in my hand"' (v.6). If so, Christ can mould me. I am a very, very small being if the house of Israel is in God's hand. If he can mould them, he can mould me. He's a big God.

Little did he know that the Heavenly Potter had nearly finished his beautiful pot, to be displayed for his glory.

John Tios later said to us, 'Pete was my friend. He humbled himself like a small child and even if we were walking from morning to night, he was still ready to preach.'

The following days were busy, so Pete didn't write much till the next Friday.

31

'How Can We Find the People Who Were Saved at Easter Time at Orus?'

This last week has been different! Thursday was the missionary prayer day at Kapropita [the missionaries of the area, from about 100 kms around, met each month in a different centre for prayer and encouragement with each other]. So, following the instructions of Mama Jeff, I drove there. However, as I needed to arrive early I went with Zachayo to Loruk the night before. I enjoyed that. Staying in the two-roomed stone/mud house of James the carpenter; walking a long way (relatively) at night to some sister's house for supper; it was good. Going to the mission prayer day was actually odd, being with wazungu [Europeans], though it was great to see the Davises and the Tinamoi team, etc.

It was his longest trip yet. From Kokwo Toto to Loruk was a journey of about 70 kilometres, and it was another 80 kilometres up that lovely hairpin-bend road to the town of Kabarnet. Kapropita was a girls' school a few miles out of town. A British missionary who was at the prayer day wrote later:

> When he gave his prayer requests, I knew at once who he was, because he sounded so like you.
>
> I was impressed by his joy and enthusiasm for what he was doing. There was no sense of tension or anxiety or problem at being in a remote place. He was full of praise for the opportunities of witnessing to the people around him and so eager to do what he could.

Two of the things he asked for prayer for were to learn more of the culture of the people and to learn more about his God. He himself added rather wistfully in his journal:

> Having much looked forward to a mzungu [European] lunch, I missed it, having to run off to Kabarnet to meet Zachayo [Kabarnet was Zachayo's home town], as prayer time finished late.
>
> We were delayed at Marigat and didn't arrive back at KT until about 9.30. Zac joked about hitting a mnyama [animal] – a jackal I let go – but one of a pair of dik-diks [small antelope] wasn't so fortunate. I have the skin now and I hope I'll be able to keep it.

He was thrilled at Marigat to be able to pick up the post – over twenty letters for Pete Jackson! Probably, he was able to get his headlight mended too. 'Friday I drove on to Orus with the full load of Davis belongings I'd picked up [presumably those he had collected in the scare two weeks earlier], helped Reuben with some work and had a slower day. We expected the Davises to arrive on Saturday, which they did.'

Art and Mary Ellen Davis, Wayne and Carol Rapp and some other friends came for the weekend. They went over to Katungura for the morning service and had a communion service there. Wayne mentioned that, unusually, he photographed Pete taking the bread, sitting between two Pokot that day. In the afternoon they climbed up the hill above Reuben's *boma* in Orus; Wayne photographed Pete against the blue background of Turkana. Pete commented in his journal:

> In the end I slept both nights in Jeff's room, and so ate all meals with them. I honestly remember thinking it strange being with wazungu again and was surprised how little the food excited me; only the pineapple was very good.
>
> Monday I began by mending one Subaru and one Land Rover puncture [this was with Wayne Rapp and they had a good time of laughter together]. Taking a 10-ply tyre off the rim is not a joke.

He had to go to Churo to collect the wives who had been evacuated earlier; the situation had settled down so well that they were all able to come back. Art went ahead to Kokwo Toto, but Pete caught up with the party to say goodbye. Wayne told me later that he could not help smiling at the huge crowd of people wanting a lift Pete had collected, all squashed into the Land Rover.

It was late when he got to Churo, about 4 p.m. He had to make arrangements for taking people for eye checks the following week, so it was too late to get back that day. After visiting Esther to tell her the news, he went to the dispensary where he happily found Zachayo too.

They stayed with the Churo dispenser, John Kamau, whom Pete described as 'a 100% sound Kikuyu'. He very much enjoyed the evening, and really felt that the prayer from Kapropita was being answered as John and another friend talked about problems and culture and Jesus. Pete realised for the first time what a burden it is for educated men like them to put all their younger brothers and sisters through school. Building a house and getting together the large dowry they need to get married have to be put off for years. People without Jesus just run off with a girl. Pete took note. 'Amazing! To learn that for Uni; to understand these people is important' – he was referring, presumably, to the importance of keeping sex within marriage.

The men were from other tribes – Tugen, Kikuyu. For the Pokot, the problem was different. Under the tribal culture, a boy is circumcised in his teens. In his early twenties he is taken through the Sapana ceremony where he has to kill an ox at one blow. At that time there is a special meeting of the community where he is given his headdress of a mud pack, and his clan helps him collect the animals he needs for a dowry to marry. But if the young man has become a Christian, no one will help. Pete learnt from Reuben that Musa's father, a very wealthy man, would not give Musa any cows, so Musa bought some goats and God prospered them, they flourished and he was able to pay his dowry. Reuben's own father had said, 'If you don't leave your religion you will have no cows from me.' But God worked a miracle for him too: Esther's parents were willing for them to marry and be paid later. Again, God blessed Reuben's animals, and his father was amazed when he saw how quickly he had gathered 30 cows! (One cow cost the equivalent of £160–£200.)

When the Davises had returned to Nairobi it seems that Pete stayed mostly with Reuben and Esther, at their invitation, at Orus. Charles and Reuben wanted him to be a companion for Reuben. For the first two weeks, as he did not have to prepare and take services for the workmen, he had more time 'to write necessary letters . . . also continue reading the pile of sound books I brought up'.

The Davises had expected him to stay in Jeff's *rondavel*, and at first he did so but then moved to their daughter's which was nearer the solar shower. But still it was about three hundred yards from Reuben's house and the *rondavel* in which the herd boy, a 14-year-old called Paulo, lived. Paulo had recently made some profession of faith, and perhaps for this reason and also because he took his meals with Reuben, Pete moved in with him. Pete always hated to look superior in any way.

The *rondavel* was another of Colin's works of three years previously. He had laid the cement base and helped erect the structure – *rondavels* come in a kit like a model kit – I think he helped erect all those at Orus. Paulo's was just across the stream from Reuben's two-roomed bungalow and other outhouses. Pete's bed was by one of the two windows, which, as the eldest, he could insist be kept open! Just outside the door was a desert rose in flower, which I'm sure Pete enjoyed. Beyond that, a curious low tree of many trunks woven together created a shady spot, where Pete no doubt often sat when Paulo had gone off with the 30-cow herd for the day; it was probably where he wrote his letters. About five yards beyond that tree, and nearer to Reuben's house, was the thorn-hedged *boma* where the cows were kept at night.

It was a busy time for driving – *'I've been to Marigat once and Kapropita once and quite a few times to Tangulbei.'* The scares of the past weeks seemed to have died down. One day, to Pete's delight, Reuben walked with him down to the plain looking for those people who had made a profession of faith at Easter. Sadly, they did not find them, but Reuben did talk to a few people they met about the Lord. They were startled by a gunshot – but did appreciate some impala meat they were brought the next day!

The big attraction of those weeks, however, was that he had time to learn more about God. He was struck very forcibly by Jeremiah 23:24, *'Do not I fill heaven and earth?'* *'He is "nearby" and "far away". The prophecy of the figs in chapter 24 actually happens. Why? Because he is a real God; he fills heaven and earth.'*

He was intrigued by an article in the December 1990 issue of *Newsweek* entitled 'Shopping for a Church', concerning the effort many American churches were making to accommodate people's tastes. 'Many clergy have simply ambushed sin out of their language. Having substituted therapy for spiritual discernment, they appeal to a nurturing God who helps his (or her) people to cope.' Mentioning the article, Pete also notes two verses: *'I am against the prophets who wag their own tongues'* (23:31) and *'Woe to the shepherds who are destroying and scattering the sheep of my pasture'* (23:1). He resolves, *'TO CONTINUE TO LEARN ABOUT THIS GOD'.*

On Saturday 6th June he read in chapter 25, *'And though the Lord has sent all his servants the prophets to you again and again, you have not listened or paid any attention.'* His thoughts turned to the wickedness in today's world and even in himself; of how pride catches one out in everything.

Pride is such a vicious circle, it is this that Christ is seen to break.

If I'm asked to speak, I'm proud – so I pray not to be but I'm proud that I pray – I speak, wondering what people think – if it's good, I'm proud, even if it's obviously the Lord.

I'm proud that I can speak, that people can ask me, that I can pray, that I'm right, that people respond, etc., etc.

I'm proud – I realise I'm proud

Where's the humble grace that God, Christ is able and that I am nothing? e.g. with the Davises I pray I'll be God-centred and yet if Mama Jeff 'hints' she is impressed, I'm proud. It's stupid writing this all out so many times but to begin to continue to see Christ, to work in me to be humble is so vital. It's the same with my 'I'm great' tendency.

I wish I had known of Pete's dilemma, for it is one I suffered from myself for months. My mother helped me enormously by telling me a prescription of the late Bishop Handley Moule, 'Take ten looks at your Saviour to every one look at yourself.'

But the Lord was teaching Pete, and had his answer.

<u>Sunday 7th June</u>
I thought today I would look up Murray's references to what Jesus worked from. In a way, to help, but also to understand the 'I am nothing/God is all' thing.

Murray states, 'The words Jesus uses describes his, Christ's, relationship to the Father.' I think *again of that* HTB [Holy Trinity Brompton, London – Rozi's church] *night long ago.*

What I understand, read, say, do, am for God, is not first – God says our relationship is.

He looked up and copied out the fourteen verses that Murray referred to – *'how Jesus just followed what God told him to do so pride could not be there. "I have come down from heaven not to do my own will but to do the will of him who sent me" (John 6:38).'*

That morning he went to church in Kokwo Toto, driving back to Orus through rain to find Esther with a painful stomach and one of Reuben's cows dead.

After dosing Esther with Kaolin [Kaolin was his father's cure-all!], *I proceeded to help Reuben cut his cow into three pieces. Hind and legs, head and legs and guts. The liver was in a terrible condition having had whitish blots all over it, pole ngombi* [poor cow]! *Having died about twenty hours previously, it was not a fresh odour. We loaded it into the back of the Land Rover and drove out, burying it in, I think, a jackal's hole. If I could make a jackal happy . . .*

He wrote a cheerful letter that week to a YWAM friend.

Never have I been so happy! No longer do people criticise or ridicule my nightwear, but about 80% of people I've met, not only wear kikois, khangas, goatskin [togas] *to bed, but all day as well . . .*

It was good hearing from your hand. After 11 very lonely weeks all was consoled in one morning, on the delivery of 20 letters which warmed my heart.

Life surely is most different from a six-month compulsory abstinence from sun, sensible companions and drink, which, however, one does occasionally recall with a touch of fondness.

He adds that his diet was mostly beans – because very few fruit and vegetables were available – so he suffered dreadfully at night from wind. Sometimes he was unable to sleep. That's part of life helping at a mission station!

Other than this, malaria, snakes, Land Rovers and mud, tropical rain, buffaloes, spears and tribal war continue to keep life exciting. The war has caused a bit of concern, particularly as guns are not hard to find nowadays, and people don't find their targets as easily as the guns. That's fine if one's a target but not if one's not.

But . . . it's been a good and rich time living with the Kenyans. I remember 'Rice-Pate' complaining about the Indian men having no hesitation about holding hands. Here, holding hands, sleeping together on a very small bed, dangling very openly if women are not around (no explanation needed) are all very normal. I, however, am not yet totally used to the habit of men, young and old, coming and stroking my slightly hairier legs and arms . . . I'm sure you would revel in it! Thankfully the church elders refrain from this.

I've enjoyed it all, though, and had time to think over the DTS days. So continue to learn, and write dumb letters to relevant people. The learning, though, has been good – what a pathetic, conceited person a PJ can be until the exchanged life is practised. . . . I haven't yet perfected this, but honestly do/am more recognising the need.

That is the soundest plan, to take a year at Oxford. (I presume this is Oxford, England, not some cheap, crummy, new, imitation Oxford elsewhere!)

Enjoy, G. bless. Be good.

One continuing proud bearer of my ancestral wear,

Pete J.

In his journal he wrote:

I think the evening after that was when two vijana [young men] came to take honey from a hive up near Reuben's cows. They were very generous with it, as normal making no effort to store any. I have never felt so sick after that, and realised only after, that I wasn't expected to eat the wax as well. The two slept with me and Paulo on the hard cement floor in the rondavel at the cow boma.

Work started again in earnest on Monday. Pete drove to Karakoi to deliver a *rondavel*, also taking patients for eye examinations by the two dispensers there. He came home the long way, by Tangulbei. Then, to his embarrassment (he wrote to tell us), he ran out of petrol in the dry river bed by the Kokwo Toto *dukas*.

But God was really answering his prayer by giving him such a thirst to learn, to know God. He had written in his journal that morning before his safari, '8th June (this time last year!)' – remembering the stark difference between school and A levels and his present circumstances. He notes that in Jeremiah 26 the prophet is threatened with death. He notes it without comment, though the events of the previous weeks may have come to his mind. What he is really interested in is how God deals with us.

Today is a definite example that God does not lay out everything. Rather, it is our choice from the freedom we're given. He says this to Jeremiah: 'Tell them everything I command you . . . Perhaps they will listen and each will turn from his evil way [their choice]. Then I will relent [God's sovereign, righteous action, depending on the choice of the people] and not bring on them the disaster [planned due to their evil],' (26: 2–3). That's to remember.

[He adds a thoughtful footnote.] It's probably worth noting, I did really make an effort to talk to/with God yesterday and whilst sitting in church I thought over the not-my-own-will/life-but-to-do-God's-will/life. I still don't know how to specifically point to it, but I realised I am not yet prepared to do that. That's quite a truth. To be a living sacrifice. My heart is not succumbed as such. I need to be and my 'top' mind says I want to be, I think I've got to/count what the bottom deep says, to Christ. That was pretty important.

Jeremiah today is calling people to reform their actions. If I do this, God fulfils his promise.

Maybe Satan had blinded him before, to the fact that if God loves us so much he will give us the best life ever. To hand ourselves to him is not only our 'reasonable service', but also the best thing to do. The Lord opened his mind to that fact that week.

On Wednesday he was reading from Jeremiah chapters 28–29:

Chapter 29 is actually a beautiful example of God's love to his people. The exiles have totally rejected God, committed adultery in his face etc, etc. God justly punishes them by sending them into exile. But, just as parents write to their children, God, through Jeremiah, sends a letter to Babylon to encourage his people. It's like the mercy; he can't just leave them/stop thinking of them.

As Floyd writes 'He dotes on us.'

'You will seek me and find me when you seek me with all your heart. I will be found by you' (29:13).

And later, '*I thought about sincerity in prayer, and then realised what I did on Sunday morning.*'

That Saturday, Pete had gone up one of the hills beside Orus. It was one of those African mornings that are out of this world.

There really is absolutely nothing as beautiful as the dawn in this continent. So quiet, with a cool breeze coming out of the valley as I sit overlooking Turkana from the hill. The birds are so beautiful. Not choruses of harmonic lullabies, but a collection of single ongoing but very different calls, out across the bush. I can only identify the emerald wood dove, yellow-necked spur fowl and a thrush, as well as various sun birds, these reminding me of Turi, Nairobi, Eldoret, Tsavo and Mombasa mornings. It's really divine . . . which is a good thing really, as finally I have come here to pray. If there is any 'motto' as such for today it's from the song I was humming as I sleepily stumbled over Reuben's thorn fence to come up here.

'My one desire' (I think still of need/desire to desire) 'is to be, holy, set aside for you, O my Father. It's to be holy, set aside for you.' ['Refiner's Fire', Brian Doerkson]

32

The Reality of the Rock:
'Endure Hardship With Us Like a Good Soldier of Christ Jesus'
(2 Timothy 2:3)

The week of Sunday 14th June got off to a dramatic start. Reuben went off on his *piki piki* (small motorbike) to visit a church. Meanwhile, as there was no regular service at Orus at that time, Pete took the Land Rover to go with Esther to the church at Kokwo Toto.

I drove out of Orus with Esther and Ches to go to KT church, only to be waved down, about 5 mins away, by the Pokot-who-makes-a-very-good-warrior. He looked anxious, though, and spoke only to Esther in Pokot, who in turn translated. At the bottom of Paka about 15 km away the Turkana had raided again and he wanted me to take him and about ten others to a hill above here to look over and out for the dust. [The mud had dried to dust again and many feet would make it rise in the air.] Esther suggested we ask Charles at KT about it. It was decided it would be good to go, so we drove. A hasty drive took us there. We stopped twice before, and at the dam to pick up about twelve warriors to fill the car. About five had guns, one a tommy, I think; whatever, it was a machine-gun.

It was an amazing thing to think what I was doing, as I hurried along the track. We descended the hill, then stopped and climbed another to look for cow dust [a herd of cows on dry earth make an impressive cloud of dust]. We saw none, and after the Pokot gave the warning cry they disappeared off into the bush. I returned with Musa. That day the local wazee, younger impressive ones in black with mud packs, met at Orus with the Administration police and the local MP himself came. It was interesting sitting under the tree with them as first one mzee rose to express his opinion then another.

People were surprised at the entrance of a warrior who came and held a spear at the MP's chest. Apparently it was to emphasise his disregard of the government's confiscation of some Pokot guns. Esther informed me that they had decided Kapedo, where the Turks came from, was to be burnt.

The excitement was put a bit into the background as I drove to Kapropita on Monday to fetch a generator . . .

It was 284 kilometres there and back. He wrote that evening, 'Flies, dust, heat and dirty, cold water make one able to be depressed . . . If I could be taught to pray . . . all the time, that would be so good. . . . then to Amaya/Churo on Tuesday for an eye clinic.'

According to Pastor Samuel of Churo, Pete stayed the night with John Kamau again that Tuesday night – a 'good evening', he wrote – but had eaten with Pastor

Elijah. Later Pastor Elijah had given Pastor Samuel a letter from Pete. It contained 500/-, with a little note to say it was to help with his car expenses, as he knew Pastor Samuel was having large repair bills. Pastor Samuel was touched and amazed that a boy could think of it. On Tuesday, Pete and the two nurses had lunch with Ray and Jill Davis at Amaya. Ray wrote, 'He was his sunny, gracious self; enjoying everyone; everyone enjoying him.'

Pete gave Pastor Samuel a lift into Tangulbei on his way home, and told the pastor, 'I must go to the duka here to get a crate of soda to put in the Davises' house, as I know they will want some when they arrive on Sunday.'

He had probably drunk several bottles of theirs when he was desperate for something sweet! But he had a very kind heart, always thinking of the little things to please people. He had written earlier to Art and Mary Ellen, thanking them for the weekend at the end of May, and added, after mentioning some tools he needed them to bring when they came on the 21st, 'More importantly, Mama Jeff [Mary Ellen], forget the ice cream [she must have promised to bring some up in her cold box]. Zachayo has never eaten pork, so a packet of bacon would be great, asante sana [thank you very much].'

There was an Irish Catholic priest stationed at Tangulbei called Father Michael. He knew Art was away, so he went up occasionally to Orus to see how things were. He met Pete that week on the roadside talking to a few Pokot. He asked him how he was.

'Thank you, I'm fine. I'm with friends, you know.'

On Saturday morning he worked for a while with Reuben to try to make the road into Orus clearer for the Davises. They moved several boulders that rain and cows had dislodged. Pete had some letters to write, but more importantly he wanted to have a last good time for prayer and take a series of photos of the great view from the top of that hill to get the whole panorama in. He managed to fix a timed one for his last shot, with himself crouched into the photo. As he would be returning to Kokwo Toto the next day he might not get another chance.

One of the letters he wrote was to his YWAM team member, Sandi Moore:

You would love it here, apart from the absence of scotch, haggis or toss-the-caber competitions, though fermented milk (for lunch today), goat's intestine (an honest regular) and spear throwing I'm sure would suffice. Other than that, 4+ inch spiders, frequent snakes, no bath or hot water, only rocks and wooden stools to relax on, unbelievable + obnoxious numbers of flies, would all continue to excite the great Scots woman of the year.

However the two most, um, interesting things are the diet and local entertainment. For one week now I've eaten a maize meal savoury porridge, drunk milk and chai from their cows and an occasional bowl of beans and maize. Fruit has been a bitter, small type of plum found wild. The entertainment has been a cattle-raiding war with the neighbouring nomadic tribe.

So Sandi, no, life is not dull. I wouldn't say it's all been one big thrill; constant flies, mosquito bites and dust do need getting used to, but boy do I/have I appreciated it. It's been an 'och of a bonnie tyme'.

Do DTS days seem many moons ago? Maybe they weren't that dull and it's been great having time to think back to cold garlic spinach, bicycle rides [Sandi's favourite] vans, Isoms, De Poorts etc., etc. Although I've been involved in church work, the biggest thing has been the personal work. Reading some awesome books and going over some of what I began to learn at DTS. So, man am I thankful for that!

And to some Dutch friends he wrote in much the same cheerful way, but added,

But I'm enjoying it, and am so thankful that the Lord has allowed me to do this for these four months . . . I miss the life of YWAM etc., though it is a good time to grow, as any growth has to be done by God only! Also, I would so like to see the church here grow. Maybe you should become missionaries here!!

I really wonder what God plans for you two, I bet it's something good. I was reading this morning that nothing is impossible for God, so was thinking he can use us for amazing things when we really look/ask him to use us. I've had a good time to rest and think about the future. I've seen it's very easy for me to say, 'God, use me in your plans' but really meaning, 'God, I'll use you for my plans', and that's so wrong. So, to learn to want nothing but God's glory.

That day up on the hill, while he was waiting for the light to be right to take his photographs, he had read from Jeremiah – he had got to chapter 31 by now – and then wrote in his journal, which had been rather neglected that week because of all the travelling. He had to use biro, which he hated, because he had left his ink in the car.

'A lesson which could easily be a repeat but shouldn't be,' he wrote thoughtfully, circling the full stop as he considered what to put next.

Jeremiah says – 'Ah Sovereign Lord, you have made the heavens and the earth by your great power, and your outstretched arm. Nothing is too hard for you.'

The Lord said, 'I am the Lord, the God of all mankind. Is anything too hard for me?'

This is in reference to God's ability to restore that broken nation. I also see things which seem so big and complex:
- Me, my pride, my apathy and incapability to go daily.
- AIC church having life and abundance of Christ.
- God doing things for people like [he mentions two names], etc.
- Just not to doubt. God is that big and can do these things. So easily.

He carefully packed up his things and went down the hill to Reuben's unfinished house as evening came on. He was quite hungry, having had only soured milk (Pokot yoghurt) for lunch.

Reuben and Paulo the herd boy told me the rest.

They all ate in Reuben's living room, sitting on locally made chairs. It was hot, as the ceiling had not yet been put in. Esther prayed for them all. Then Pete and Paulo went peacefully to bed, in the *rondavel* across the dry

stream bed. In the weeks before, many Pokot scouts
had been out watching for retaliating Turkana, but as
the Turkana had raided Kinyang the week before, at
full moon, now there were hardly any scouts on duty.

That night, about three hundred Turkana *ngoroko*
moved silently up the valley to Kokwo Toto, some
even to Tangulbei – a four hundred square mile area.
They collected 3,000 cows and killed a woman and two
children in Kokwo Toto, then came sweeping back down
the Orus valley at about 5 o'clock in the morning.

Paulo and Pete were woken by two gunshots fired
into the air up by the Davises' house. Then a face
appeared at Pete's open window. Two men broke down
the door. One of them caught Paulo by his *shuka* and
lifted his spear to kill him, but it hit the roof of the hut,
so he lost momentum. Paulo grabbed the opportunity
and slipped out of his *shuka* and out of the door. There
were three more Turkana at the door, but he slipped
round the back and tore his bare feet to shreds running
on the hills behind Orus until he almost got to Kokwo
Toto. As he ran, he called on God to help him.

The other Turkana had a gun. As Paulo had escaped,
he turned on Pete.

Paulo heard Pete speak quietly and firmly to the
men. One of them replied. Then he heard two shots.

Pete gave a great shout and, because of the blood of
the Jesus who had died for him 2,000 years before, he
stepped straight into the presence of his Deliverer; in
the triumph of a life 'that shall endless be'.

33

Weeping With One Eye:
'A Servant is Not Above His Master'

It had to come. It always does. The question was: what
to do with Pete's 'jar of clay', his 'tent', his body? It
was very special – God-made, God-grown, God-died-
for, similar to the one God himself clothed himself in
when he came to deliver us from Satan. Because Pete
had received life from Jesus, his body was not just a
dead seed, but one with life in it that will be incredibly
changed when that last trumpet gets going, just in one
twinkle of an eye!

Julian and I, Jonathan, Sharon, Rozi and Colin met
at Jonathan's home in East Dulwich to make decisions.
Because so many from Pete's old school wished to be
with us at the funeral, our vicar had encouraged us to
bury Pete in England. He would probably have wanted
to be buried in Kenya but we felt it was right to bring
his body back – and it was possible because of Pete's
insurance.

We drove to Emmanuel Church, South Croydon, for
the service. I had bought a new pink-flowered dress. It
was not a time for mourning – certainly not mourning
in the heathen sense. We knew that many of our dear
family were coming, but we were awed by the sight of

so many people streaming through those grey doors. Among them were thirty-six Tonbridge schoolboys, even though it was holiday time, and some of their parents came. What were you doing that day, Lord? I think we'll know in heaven.

We also held two memorial services in Kenya. One was at Orus, sitting round the tree right outside the *rondavel* from where Pete had been taken. Loving friends came to sit with us, many from great distances; we do not forget them. Some Pokot came, and were puzzled and amazed that we did not want revenge on the killers. They themselves had walked through that day and night of the 21st, and had caught up with the raiding party, retrieved the cattle and killed ten of the raiders.

'Do you see this tree with many trunks?' Edward Limo asked. 'It will be the same with Pete; many trunks will come from that one. Pete's work will be like that. There will be many young people who will raid this country with the gospel.' Later a young Pokot student told us, 'You were expecting Pete would give you *grands* [grandchildren]. You will have many *grands* here.'

The second service was at Ziwani. Over a thousand people gathered there to be with us. We were encouraged by what the Kenyans told us there, too. An elder who knew Pete well said to me, 'You know, in the womb all the eggs cry when a baby leaves, but outside we are all rejoicing in a new child. It's the same with heaven.'

The AIC bishop in his address said, 'At home, if a man is killed in battle we say we only cry with one eye, because it is a great honour. Pete died in battle for Jesus.'

Peter Kanyi, who had been such a great family friend, told us that he was really sad at first when he knew we had taken Pete's body back to England.

Then he remembered that his blood was in Kenya. The blood is the person. At the Ziwani memorial service he stood up and gave a rousing cry to young Kenyans – of whom there were many in the church – to take up Pete's place, to tell other Kenyans about Jesus. We have met several young people since then whose lives were turned round to be full time for Jesus that day. Many people, too, have written us wonderful letters of encouragement. I quote from just two of them: 'Pete once said that if he should find out his life would end tomorrow, then he could only feel happiness, since he knew where he was headed' (Karl and Rupert). 'Do not have any sense of guilt for allowing him to go there. What I saw was not a child, but a young man, totally fulfilled in his love for the Lord and joy in serving him' (Violet Culliford, who saw Pete at the prayer meeting three weeks before he died).

Yet the cry of many people was, 'Why? Why? Why, Lord?'

I have been slowly coming to realise that we so often have a wrong view of what being a Christian is all about. We pick out a few Bible verses and we ignore others. We praise God when everything goes well, and we say 'How awful' about anything sad.

I think Pete had known since he was a child that to follow Jesus meant to be a soldier. Jesus said, *'You call me "Master" and "Lord", and you do well to say it, for it is true'* (John 13:13 TLB).

'The student shares his teacher's fate. The servant shares his master's' (Matthew 10:25 TLB).

In his first Bible (the Good News Version) Pete underlined, with a wobbly pencil line, *'For whoever wants to save his own life will lose it, but whoever loses his life for my sake will save it'* (Luke 9:24).

We all have to die. And the question we have to ask is not 'When?' or 'How?', but 'For what purpose?' – Will I die for money? Will I die for fame? Will I die for gardening, or indeed for any selfish thing?

34

Postscript

Two years later we went back to Orus, for the dedication of a small grey breezeblock church that had been built on the rise above the Davises' house in Pete's memory. It had been made possible through the kindness of an American newscaster, Dini Petty. Many Pokot travelled from a distance to be with us; some came in their beads, mud caps and feathers. Church leaders from the region also came.

Part of the service was set aside for a time of praise. Person after person stood up to share their thoughts – 'The wonderful way this church was built, because of Pete's death' . . . 'This place was bushy, God is now shining his light here.'

Jonathan Hildebrandt spoke of Peter Cameron Scot, the young man who, a hundred years ago, died after only eighteen months in Kenya – but whose vision was the origin of the large Africa Inland Church that now exists in Kenya. He said, 'May the Lord who planted the grain of wheat at Pete Jackson's death bring a great harvest here also.'

My eyes filled with tears as ten ladies from Orus got up to sing. Many of them had become Christians in the previous two years. Esther, Reuben's wife, led them. She said, 'We know Pete is in heaven, because he believed in Jesus.' They sang a glorious staccato Pokot song. Jill Davis whispered to me, 'It is based on the words, "There is life, alleluia! If you follow Jesus, you will go to heaven – alleluia!".'

One of the evangelists spoke next:

'In Pokot culture, it's taboo to remember the name of someone who has died. We are so glad the disciples did not believe that about Jesus! Pete is alive, and he will rise again. It's the best news you can give a Pokot – that someone has risen again.'

I spoke a few words, and then Julian spoke.

'God promises to keep the feet of these who love him. He promises us protection, and it is right to pray for it. But God is the President of all Presidents. We didn't want our child to die, but God chooses the time we must go. Yet it is not real death if we believe in Jesus, because he brings us life.

'Do not fear death. It is only like the strings of beads some Indians have hanging in their doorways – you just touch them and enter into their homes. But God warns us to be fearful of the second death – the real separation of those who do not believe in Jesus (Revelation 2:11).'

We stood up stiffly from sitting on the wooden benches and shook hands with everybody. Then we went out into the sunshine wondering what the Lord would do next.

We have heard of some of the things God has done.

Reuben told us that in the years following Pete's death, there was a new openness to the gospel in that area around Orus and some Pokot had begun turning to Jesus.

In the year 2000 there was another severe drought. The herdsmen took their cattle miles down onto that great plain again, Turkana or no Turkana, for grass. Art asked an organisation that flew helicopters to help the evangelists, and as they flew them from place to place where they saw the herds, many Pokot men came to the Lord.

Paulo, who had turned away from the Lord after his ordeal that night of 21st July 1992, was convicted again after the third time the helicopter had come down where his herd had moved to. The following day he walked for four hours up to Orus to meet the Christians who prayed together at 8 a.m. He told them, 'Tell Pete Jackson's parents that their prayers have been answered; I've come back to God and want to study to be an evangelist.'

Also, many people have told us that hearing or reading of Pete's death has challenged them to go for Jesus in a new way. One man told me, 'We've called our son Peter because we wanted him to have a hero to follow.'

From the memorial fund that was set up in memory of Pete, quite a number of Pokot and Turkana pastors have been trained.

My eldest sister, Mollie, sent us her Bible study notes for the month of June 1992, which were based on the book of Job, showing that the problems Job was facing on earth were actually part of a big confrontation in heaven between God and Satan. Then a friend wrote, 'I think God was doing something much bigger, as in Ephesians 3:10–11: *"His intent was that now, through the church, the manifold wisdom of God should be made known to the rulers and authorities in the heavenly realms, according to his eternal purpose which he accomplished in Christ Jesus our Lord."* He was revealing through Pete something to the heavenly realms.' I was very encouraged.

The Sunday after Pete was taken to heaven, we felt we could not face our friends, so we went to a London church. John Peters spoke on 2 Corinthians 4; it was a huge comfort:

> *This is for your benefit, so that the grace that is reaching more and more people may cause thanksgiving to overflow to the glory of God. Therefore we do not lose heart. Though outwardly we are wasting away, yet inwardly we are being renewed day by day. For our light and momentary troubles are achieving for us an eternal glory that far outweighs them all* (2 Corinthians 4:15–17).

For those who believe in Jesus, '*Death has been swallowed up in victory*' (1 Corinthians 15:54). Yes!

Glossary of Swahili Words

Asante sana	Thank you very much
Bandas	Small two-roomed stone huts, which provided the basic necessities of life
Boma	Byre. As well as its meaning of a cow byre or animal compound, a *boma* – usually an area enclosed by thorn-tree branches or a fence – can be a place where a family lives, with a house for each wife and teenage child, and store houses.
Chai	Tea (refers here to a local brew of tea leaves, sugar and milk boiled together)
Chakula	Food
Chakula ngini	Bad Swahili! But means 'more food'
Chombo	A vessel
Choo	Toilet
Dawa	Medicine

Dukas	Small shops originally run by Indians, but now mostly by Kenyans
Fundi	Somebody who is an expert in his or her field
Githeri	A heavy bean and maize mixture
Hajabu	Amazing, miraculous
Hoteli	Hotel, restaurant or tea shop
Iko mzuri	It's good
Itakuwa mzuri	It will/would be good
Jaa	Full
Jambo	A Swahili greeting that means 'What's the affair?' it is the Kenyan 'Hello'
Kabisa	Completely, absolutely
Kahawa	Coffee
Kazi	Work
Kiboko	Hippo
Kidogo	Small, little
Kikoi	A Kenyan striped cloth worn by men at the coast, popular with tourists
Kuanza	To start with
Kumbe!	A Swahili exclamation
Kwaheri	Goodbye
Mafuta	Oil or petrol
Maneno	Discussion, debate, consultation, argument
Mandazi	A type of Kenyan doughnut
Matatu	A form of private transport in Kenya, usually a minibus or covered pick-up, whose drivers are usually a law to themselves on the road and drive furiously
Mazuri tu	Just good

Mbao	Planks of wood
Mlam Tich	The place where the-cows-never-go-hungry
Mlimi	A high hill
Mnyama	Animal
Mungu	God
Mstuni	The bush
Musa na mimi	I/me
Mzee	Old man, elder
Mzungu	European/white person
Ngoroko	Raiders
Ni hajabu	Out of this world, miraculous
Nimeshangaa	I was amazed, astonished
Ni safi, Bwana	It's excellent, Mister
Peke yake	On my own
Pole	My very deep sympathies
Pole ngombi	Poor cow
Pole sana	I felt very sorry for them
Rondavel	A prefabricated round metal hut, as used by the Roads Department
Safi	Clean or excellent
Safi sana	Really good
Sasa ni karibu ya	Now it's nearly
Shuka	Cloth worn by men
Stima	Electricity
Terungi stop	Tea break (*terungi* is tea without milk)
Ugali	Thick, mashed potato type of dish made from boiled maize meal
Vibarua	Casual labourers
Vijana	Young men
Wazee	A term of respect for elderly people
Wazungu	Europeans/white people

Notes

1. C.S. Lewis, *Till We Have Faces: A Myth Retold* (Geoffrey Bles, 1956)
2. Jonathan Goforth (1859–1936) in *By My Spirit* described the remarkable revivals that occurred in China in the early twentieth century.
3. Many Indians had been brought to Kenya by the British around 1885 to help build the railway from the coast to Uganda. Many of the families decided to settle in Kenya, where today there is still an Asian community.
4. Many private schools in England have the house system. Tonbridge School's approximately 625 boys were divided into ten 'houses'. They lived in their 'house' for their whole school career, meeting the rest of the school for classes and games. Pete was in Judde House.
5. Spring Harvest is an annual Christian conference held in several locations in England. They are based in Butlins holiday camps. There are meetings and seminars for all age groups, and thousands attend each year.
6. Many boys' boarding schools in England run clubs for the Army, Navy and Airforce. They are called Corps. Pete had chosen to join the one for the Navy.
7. Paul Yonggi Cho, *Prayer: Key to Revival* (Word Publishing, 1984).

8. As well as its meaning of a cow byre or animal compound, a *boma* – usually an area enclosed by thorn-tree branches or a fence – can be a place where a family lives, with a house for each wife and teenage child, and store houses.

9. A term of honour given to one who had completed four years of secondary education. Others would be called a 'Form 2 leaver', etc.

Twenty years have gone by since this book was written. We thank God that at least ten people were trained as pastors with the money donated at Pete's death. So we praise God for the continued witness from Pete's death to Jesus in Kenya. Also in Uganda, a centre for healing for traumatised child soldiers has been named after him. We thank God that our life and death are not in vain when we follow our living master Jesus.

Rachel Jackson, May 2012